THE ANABRANCH

Newcastle Poetry Prize
Anthology 2022

THE UNIVERSITY OF NEWCASTLE AUSTRALIA

HUNTER WRITERS CENTRE

The Anabranch
Newcastle Poetry Prize Anthology 2022

Hunter Writers Centre Inc. and the University of Newcastle
Newcastle NSW 2300

Published by
Hunter Writers Centre inc.
hunterwriterscentre.org

ISBN-978-0-6488504-9-6

Cover design by Renee McIntosh
Typesetting by HWC Publishing
2022 Published by Hunter Writers Centre Inc.

When I first hear about the Anabranch it is already a poem,
a magic word in my mind.

~ Claire Albrecht
The Anabranch
Winner 2022 Newcastle Poetry Prize

Contents

Introduction viii

~ Winner, 2022 Newcastle Poetry Prize ~
The Anabranch 12
Claire Albrecht

~ 2nd Prize ~
A Letter to the Judges 16
Christopher (Kit) Kelen

~ 3rd Prize ~
Scrumdingling 24
Leigh Jordan

~ Commended ~
Recent sightings of Tito 26
Jennifer Kornberger

~ Commended ~
Sanatorium 33
Jakob Ziguras

~ Local Award ~
Five Elegies 45
David Bruce Musgrave

~ Harri Jones Prize for a Poet under 36 years ~
A Life of Prizes 52
Dan Hogan

emptiness, nulls, *nullius* 54
Syd Daniels

Haiku Variations 60
Asiel Adan Sanchez

in the interest of clarity 62
Christine Fontana

Hard Work 66
Shelley Wylie

Abstract Silence [a] 72
Aleph

Abstract Silence [c] 73
Aleph

Gimbay Wanggal (Friendship Dance) 74
Nicole Smede

Rain Lillies 76
Kerry Greer

Commission Home 79
Kevin Smith

READY? 82
Greg McLaren

All Week the Early Skies 87
Mark Tredinnick

Goodbye Look 90
John Hawke

the cost price of a flaming gala 94
Dave Drayton

Cooks River Canal — Wangal Country, 1990s 96
Dimitra Harvey

Building the Coffin 98
Coral Carter

Bait Balls 100
Sara Crane

Originary 101
Anne M Carson

Flirting in Norwegian 108
Jenny Pollak

Anthology 111
Anthony Lawrence

Princess was here 117
Tim Ungaro

Intents 129
Anne Elvey

Vertigo 134
John Kinsella

Red 139
Larisa Jacono

Halls Creek Road 141
Glenn McPherson

Requiem for Ronald McDonald 143
Damen O'Brien

Coffins 147
Verity Oswin

The extravagant rectitude of bees 149
John Kinsella

Introduction

This anthology takes its title from the prize-winning poem, 'The Anabranch'. An anabranch is a section of river that diverts from the main channel that it then re-joins further downstream.

Each poem in this anthology is an anabranch in itself—a deviation from the mainstream; a moment where time would seem to stand still; a 'stay against the confusion of the world,' in Robert Frost's memorable phrasing. There is something anabranch-ish about our moment, as our deviation from what life was in 2020 reconnects further downstream in 2022. Rivers moved from drought to fullness to flood. Our communities were pushed and pulled either side of the poverty line. We oscillated between an open world and isolation.

It is hardly the same river, but it is—more's the pity—pulling us inexorably in the same direction, and it appears an opportune time to take stock. How should we look towards this new future, which we arrived upon as surprisingly as the disruptions of 2020-21? How should we reflect upon our recent and distant pasts while the present is so clearly marking history? The poems in this anthology grapple with these questions, among others.

It has been a pleasure to judge the Newcastle Poetry Prize. Over the course of a month, we read, re-read and reflected upon the hundreds of entries. Neither of us have read so many poems in a single month—and certainly neither of us have read poetry by a greater number of diverse poets in such a short time frame. Our reading provided a fascinating snapshot of poetry as it is being written here in 2022—in its near-infinite variety of purposes, themes and forms.

We have tried as far as possible to judge each poem on its own terms, favouring no mode of writing, and we have aimed in our selection to represent the variety of forms and themes we saw in the poems submitted. The judging took place over five rounds. The first round produced a list of just over one hundred poems that one or both of us thought potentially worthy of inclusion in an anthology. The final two meetings decided our prize-winning poems and the commendations. Many noteworthy poems we received are not in this anthology. Of the poems that came close to inclusion, often an otherwise impressive poem was marred by a weak stanza or section, a tension was broken too soon, or a sputtering opening weakened something that was otherwise powerful. These are, perhaps, unsurprising in longer works, of which there were many. Some of our judgments have, doubtless, been in error and only our own personal taste—either shared or negotiated—can account for this.

The three poems we regarded most highly changed places a number of times, but as we read and re-read them, and weighed up their qualities, we decided that 'The Anabranch' by Claire Albrecht was our winner.

'When I first hear about the Anabranch it is already a poem', the speaker tells us in the opening section, and what such a poem that might be is explored through the dream world and the material world, in its ideal and real forms. 'The Anabranch' defies characterisation. Its themes, appropriately, diverge and converge; its concerns are manifold—environmental but also aesthetic, metaphysical and epistemological. This poem delighted us with its richly suggestive and memorable phrasing, and we were surprised to find new interpretative possibilities at each reading. The author's control of tone is flawless, yet the surface is often roughened by the snags lurking below. It was especially gratifying to discover, after the names were revealed, that this poem was written by one of the competition's younger entrants.

Our runner-up, 'A Letter to the Judges' by Kit Kelen, was particularly bold in its direct address to us. This substantial and sure-footed poem was the funniest we read and the most self-reflexive. There is no tang of the schoolroom about the remarkable erudition, and the brilliant wit nicely leavens the poem's formidable technical vocabulary. The dizzying array of literary reference is often double-edged, and the occasion of the poem's knowing construction is an opportunity to more broadly reflect upon our moment in political, social and literary terms—the centres that are not holding, the multiple tracks on which a poem might run.

'Scrumdingling' by Leigh Jordan, our choice for third place, was an excursion into the world of the dog as a way of thinking about a poem in itself. A poem of joyous linguistic play, 'Scrumdingling' is overloaded with sensuous detail, providing a perspective different to any other entry. It is witty and self-aware, and its charming humour is never cute or sentimental. The poem's rhythms are expertly controlled and sustained through to its exuberant and memorable resolution: 'He knows, as mere observers / we dare not / look back!'

We have awarded the local prize to 'Five Elegies' by David Musgrave, a poem that eloquently contemplates the void left by loss. 'A Life of Prizes' by Dan Hogan, a mosaic of fragments of time and space broken up by tech capitalism, was our choice for the Harri Jones prize. These poems also received commendations. Two further commendations go to 'Recent Sightings of Tito' by Jennifer Kornberger and 'Sanatorium' by Jakob Ziguras, both highly compelling and technically exquisite monuments to their subjects.

We would like to thank the Hunter Writers Centre for all the help and guidance. We especially thank Professor Mark Hoffman, DVC (Academic) of the University of Newcastle for the ongoing support of poetry in Australia through the significant prize money. And we thank the contributors. It has been an honour and a pleasure to have judged this venerable prize. We hope readers relish this selection as much as we have enjoyed compiling it.

Alison Whittaker and Aidan Coleman

The Anabranch

Claire Albrecht

I dream about the Anabranch again. Luminous tubes at high speed. Like *F Zero X* on the Nintendo 64. But it's nothing like that. You wouldn't even know it was there, but for the blue hydrants along the highway. Popping up like buds in the spring to greet the baby emus. Fluff meets iron. When I first hear about the Anabranch it is already a poem, a magic word in my mind. I will dream about it every night for three weeks.

The Anabranch begins, really, where everything begins: the sky. But for now let's call it the Severn. And in the belly of the Severn, right now, is the idea of a Golden Perch. Glinting. Conceiving of itself as the Billy Bass in your bathroom sings and wiggles. This idea catches the sun and moves downstream, flowing into the Darling, catching on floodwater, skidding along as the banks are taken over.

If you think of water administrators as gods, you'll begin to get the idea. Today my psychologist asked me to identify what the words 'restrict' and 'allow' have in common. My answer should have been the Anabranch, but it wasn't on his list. These thoughts follow different river beds.

The colours here are bonkers. Out of reckoning. I want to wear a dress of the desert but I can't even take a photograph. Tufts of golden emu doing their thing against purple saltbush, bluebush, silvertail, red dirt, blue sky. A different palette of water colour. I pull the scenes in with my eyelids, hungry.

The Anabranch is named for its refusal to diverge. An un-splitting. The anastomosis opens. The blood stream opens. A surgeon makes a connection. On Lake Cawndilla, the anastomosis opens and closes at the outlet on a whim. Five years ago, it shut. There is no real antonym, only words like disconnection. The Anabranch hadn't paid the bills.

Remember that idea? The glimmering, golden one? It's in the Barka, that Darling, and is merging with the reality of a golden perch. A yellowbelly. A slimy little egg. The big brown waters flush it through, spiralling down and down over the old riverbeds drinking up all the good stuff and spitting our golden guy out into the lakes. With old memories of trees sticking up like a stork dance arrested.

The Anabranch is a big deal here and nowhere else. The best roads go along the Anabranch. The cormorants all know the Anabranch, the grebes and white herons. Between Mungo National Park and the Lakes, it's all Anabranch. Usually all dust. The ants all know the Anabranch too. Knowing the Anabranch is like knowing life and death, the postal system, the poker table. The precise Revlon red of your grandmother's daily lipstick.

I nearly ran out of petrol the first time I went to find the Anabranch. Coasting down towards Wentworth with a flavour for risk, I bet it all on the Coombah Truckstop and lost. Doors locked, pumps dry. Mr Henderson in hospital, a blue Hilux told me. I coasted my way back the Silver City snakeway like a golden perch in a river smoking cigarettes. Glistening with sweat and slippery on the seat.

Our little egg is becoming a little fish, wriggling about and bursting into golden lakeform. The shingleback lizard steps into the middle of the road and tastes the air. The goanna climbs from its perch and tastes the air. The bearded dragon makes a pattern in the sand and tastes the air. Our golden fish tastes water for the first time, and its eyes bulge.

When I finally find the Anabranch, I have had to come at it from a different angle. Winding along windows down through Kinchega National Park I am unphased by the dry white skeletons along the roadside. They are from a before that doesn't live here anymore. The grasses have grown up and through them, water pooling around the past. I stop my car on a small bridge, birds take flight, I turn off the music and walk on water. I am above, I am in, I belong to the Anabranch.

How could I have known that when I passed the Cawndilla outlet, where the Paakantji fellas are fishing at the gush, that my path had begun to cross with our perch. This little fish, miraculous in itself, has made it to a river that doesn't always exist. Some other year, the idea of this fish might have dried up just like the rest. Bird food in the lake bed. But its yellow belly is growing fat and flourishing. We are in our element.

In a little cottage on Sunset Strip I drink and dance the solitude, watching the colours crease across the water, summoned up above tree roots and parchwork and abandoned jetskis. A man tries his reel at the shuffling shoreline. At night the waves crashing against branches replace the white noise I play on my phone. The anonymity of being alone is a turn-on. My own golden belly moves in the eventual darkness.

Our perch plans a long and glistening life. She doesn't know it, but she could survive until her mid twenties, learning every movement of the Barka. As she flies past the sleeping Coombah Truckstop, past the emu-ruffled pastures, she is unaware of her own miracle. The very scales are articles of history already. They protest again closure, against restraint, against ownership. A promise of life rumbles inside her, profound and inevitable.

Where the Barka both splits and unifies, a small lane runs off the highway. I had stopped my car to capture the junction, to light a smoke and muddy my boots at the original couplet. The Murray and Darling balcony scene. The boardwalk was closed from the flooding. I wiped my boots, held in a river of piss, and started up the car. The river has no time for photographs.

Our golden perch is absolutely loving herself. She dances into Mildura, flashing sequins under the lights of houseboats and hanging willow. A celebrity chef is serving lamb in the restaurant under the casino, and the Italian server is telling me that they would never bother with lamb where she's from. She is pouring me a stream of wine; she thinks I am a restaurant critic. I am fish-drunk and playing my role. Later, stumbling riverside, I consider submerging entirely. Two perch eyes, small and stunned in the dark, bear witness.

In reports on golden perch and the impact of water regulation on their breeding patterns, the aim is clear: produce conditions for more fish, so that there may be more fishing. The purpose of the noun is the verb. A self-sustaining prophecy. The Anabranch is a temporary blood vessel. The supply can be cut off at any time. Surgical intervention hovers like a net. This fish lives, the others will die. Most will not be born. The fisheries will fail. Perch will be raised in hatcheries and farmed out to dams to die. What the fuck are they doing out there?

There is something Anabranchy about a poem. The way it comes and goes, being so clear for a moment (like: of course, how else?) then retreating back to bed. Once unleashed, it knows the path it will follow, and takes the dust along with it. It doesn't care about the years of drought before it, just finds gaps in meaning to fill. There will always be more gaps. There will always be the Anabranch, and it will mostly be empty, and as I drive away to the east my mouth is dry, my skin is burning.

A Letter to the Judges

Christopher (Kit) Kelen

ONE

You won't believe this. Or maybe you will. Or grudgingly. Whatever.
It's not my job to make you happy. I've spread myself too thin already.

I do think you should entertain it though, in all conscience, at least for
the sake of entertainment. You won't get rid of me without odd pangs.

I'm going to write this next year too. Only you won't read it then. Unless
it gets in. It probably won't. Whose loss? Some people buy scratchies.

You have to admire the cussed persistence of the poem, to have itself
rewritten every year like this. And here's a poet, has to be, *trompe l'oeil*,

as it were, avowing this will be done for as long as it takes. I will will it
to my offspring, even unto the seventh son/daughter, of the seventh, and so on.

(How can you know I haven't inherited it myself?... Isn't it as if we were
always here, me with these lines endlessly shaped, you with this silly dare?)

Let it be recorded in whichever heaven you like, I have a poem to smoke
to the ancestors, to raise beaker with, take pills for, be bound to that juggernaut

revision, until it's past the post and placed, and/or more likely, also ran.

O weep but a little for this dross,
I won't be cross.

Platonist improvisation. Mirror faceted, and ask, which poem is the original (?)

It is a series of tests I have set. If you kill it now, can it ever improve?
The reflex poem. Covid conditions persist. The knee-jerk reaction, precautions.

One future of democracy is in these shaking hands. Your mission
should you choose to accept it, (and my mission too) to fall
like sunlight merely, over the object of interest.

TWO
That's the first strophe in the bag. Too easy, as they say.
I suppose I should have started with a 'Dear somebody-or-other, ...'
Too late now. Here's poetaster lowering tone again.

Like dog's balls or an intentional fallacy. Licked either way. A little one-
sided as conversation goes; a letter is a kind of ode, if you have a think.
But then two poems might meet discreetly. (It happens all the time.

Where do you think poems come from?) And as with much romance,
it's hard to see why it's not prose; sometimes you just have to have faith.
'Believe me.' (That was Fats Waller.) I write from the heart. The head itself

cannot make poetry, however handy. And yet the head is top
of the tree. And coconut too. Want a wrestle? Howsabout
hide-n-seek, a board game? Or let's canoe? Come out of hiding.

You know this voice, don't you? Don't you know all the voices?
Or you want it to be a stranger? You want to be a stranger yourself?
Prosopopoeia! Fresh joy in masks and unmasking. Lavish of throwing voice.

Being thrown by it. And double dare ya. You can just stop reading. Wipe.
Kill this thing off now. There isn't a duty to go on. Only 800 entries to go.

STROPHE THE THIRD
Still here? I hear a stifled moan. Wotsup? Is that pain or approbation?

There is a time limit for the writing of the letter. Not imposed
by rigid fear, but product of anxiety. We too, you see, have rules,
of a sort. You only go at it when you want. So it has to be
the honest truth. Many of us are at work in this way. It is a baring
of life and limb to all the colour we can muster. There are numbers
on the backs of our cards. CVC—what's this? But we know now.
We hammer the tongs, by tooth and nail, as hoist to own petard.

Never learn our lesson. (We're paying, so why not bunch the titles up?)
YES, NATURE … it is a highly allusive system, everything connects.
Rhizomatically is cool. Prayer's a filibuster.

Based on observation—valley shaped to sun, little wonder of a cloud,
but now the moon must mist. See cattle, hear the *fark fark* crows.
I like to gather in the wood then. Stack branches. All these tasks to laud.

In the vizier's garden, a dry sierra. That orchard trickle of the past is dust.

All through the sun, and the billowing sails
fish in the net flap silver, gold.

The last two centuries? Who needs 'em? Be sublime.

Say 'delicate'—you've done your dash. Make twee. With dappled dulcet zeal.
Might as well have 'cerulean', 'petrichor'—'effulgent'.

Shockers! Yet gong to smartypants won't go.
By the time you read this though, the wicked Tories may be done.

SQUEAL NOW (Mainly it's the sins of the fathers.)
Or something more evocative. There has to be urban grit
in the works. His slutty face, her leer. And the bodies later

with whom cause shall not attribute. Detective poem?
The future grammar is imagined. Can't be a pretty sight;

not for us in our nowadays nighties. We've forgotten years.
Just as the ideal map exceeds territory in scope,

the poem can never be more than a plan of/for itself.
And of its time, and limits, telling—living work.

Rhetorical knockout punch somewhere round here.
Lines to ring forever, like pennies in a till.

STROPHE THE NEXT
Is it a journey? (Yes, we're working through a list.)
Could be a walk across the empty city. The Hill or Cook's Hill.
Let's not give too much away. Say Merewether Baths to Nobby's,
few lattes, swim, bit of a chat, best part of a day. Our ocean was allowed.
Why do people live anywhere else? (A: So we might pity them.)
And industry's out there, still queuing on the horizon.
Coal! The future's going to be the past. They're breathing this
in India now (And some must breathe their last) … No,
it's too ponderous to tell. Which centre cannot hold?

Parts of the poem should seem still like draft …

rhymes buried and long rhymes too, this could be dictation,
automatic writing, the epistolary italic, aliens in the anthology

(and just as suddenly, the punctuation's back, if erratic though).
Effort of months/of years to seem dashed off as if last minute,
to a deadline … True pride of craft self-deprecates.

Struggle to strike right note. Somewhere between Dryden and Pope.
Balmain needs harrowing again. Glad to have got that out of the way.

Refrain ?
Yes, praps you wish I had. So pencil in some indignation.
I write out of moral responsibility. Witness all kinds of vanishing.

Economy, for instance. It's the war on the world I don't get. And on the trees!
It's every lie was white once. Are there Nazis in Ukraine? Yes, and in Moscow too.
Nazis are everywhere. Here, try this spray. It's good beyond the grave.

NEXT SECTION BAROQUE (with 'Ventilator Blues')
The noun phrase, like expanded territory—a season end to it.
The poem is concertina; every world is filed somewhere. Spuds under 'P'.
There's 'handle'—that's 'off which to fly'. Want pandering, do you?

Another artform or narrative of voyage, this day containing all others before.

We're somebody else's exoplanet. Suck *that* up, you fool. Un-pun!

CONFIDE AND THREATEN (in Dale Carnegie's sinister cypher)
I know about … the accident (so-called) and the letter (dodgy hand),
the deleted messages … Who do you think you are and what gives you
the right? Is there such a thing as a *safe* secret? Ah, but there's nothing that
must really spill. Destiny is in your hands if we can agree to terms.

APOLOGIA
Forgive this last outburst. Of course I accept your what-shall-we-say (?)
unreservedly unconditionally anonymously, etceterally.

Or are we just a little superstitious, game to leave this out?
Shortlist's the only way to know. Good oil that you can trust.

You'd think a letter had a middle; this simply isn't true.
There's a moment though you know you're well past. Symmetry
must be defied. Belly ache or belly laugh? Even if
you should decide you wouldn't be able to tell.

EPIGRAMMATIC

Go to bed and the day's still in us.

So many are birds, those of the air—
there must be a trick to it.

In little wildernesses of the missive,
where grief outpours the heart to live—
ask, would women ever love (?). Did men?

Obscurity—the dark will choose us.

In trouble for being cheerful again?
Don't get into the Bible that way.

IN AUTOBIOGRAPHIC MODE

The poet with the specimen box collecting wilds of her own mind,
just to be generic. It's like the idiot in the story and just don't get it
about cliques and bubble ambition, vanity of human wishes, the poetry
compulsion—clinical variety. Once friend of mine tried to stop—poet I mean—
churns out the good stuff. Was so sickened by how it all goes; thought what's
the point (?). Made a month on the poetry waggon and then began to feel
physically ill from not making. Realized poetry's something you do
for the sake of a little lie down. Have to give yourself the guernsey.

It's like managing sex urges of the upper primates. Will not be done remotely,
but we lure them in. There are about five hundred in this country—seriously
afflicted. How contagious? It's hard to say. Never seems to catch on. Next.

Shake my hand and double your dole. (Limited period offer). That was Hawaii Smoko
of the eleven million hectares. Has to be dated for a footnote later. Then there
were the floods. And go again. A catalogue of lies. What's carbon footprint of a war?
All oil. One in five deaths worldwide now are smog, did you know? Seven mill. Play market
yo-yo. Blow up a sacred site. Have another? Here's old growth. The koalas and me still.

Do lives matter? **ANTISTROPHE** around about here.
It could simply be a question of losing count. And yet the poet
keeps toting up lines! As if they were Noble Numbers. You bet!

Lip twitch of herpes or an itchy arse. The hip that tells of autumn,
as ants of rain. Once the ache gets in, like rats in the rafters, hell to be rid of.

You ask after my health? That's kind. Might be form
or you're just trying to be funny. The ringing in the ears won't stop.

One could grizzle one's tits off in a letter like this
and where would that get us? Torn between two genres, more,

feeling like our work's to get thing all measured.
How many tracks can the poem run on? You tell me.

You can do it in the speech. No one'll mind much and here I am
getting a tedious job out of the way for you. How many poems

are as helpful as this? How can you think I'm not owed?
Poetry's grim reaper too. Or else—your time will come!

It's the thing you think won't fit that makes it,
sets the whole thing snug.

EPODE

Swear out an affidavit that all the words are mine. Because
anyone could have written this. I'll see you in the O.E.D.
That's what you have to bear in mind. How can we believe
though? Committing words to paper as such, can't be sure
that I'm alive. I could be wraith here for appearance … Dark vanishing,
fully Victorian; if it wasn't for the breathy patches … Pinch and Tickle.
(Solicitors.) Two hundred lines is a fair whack of frame.

The forms defy coherence. I become a school.
And swim for it. Sunlight's for the treetops now.

Assume there must be an ending somewhere though possibly *in media res*.
Hard to catch a coda when you've swallowed your own tail.
(Great garbage patch now *in* the fish. Look just like single-use soy.)

Nietszche, when he was most mad, then wished to be understood.
A few of us have got this, like we're where light lasts. You could make
your way by just a dim poet once. Too much photopollution now. Things
were twiddly in the ancient days, now they call that steampunk. Sigh.
And LOL, he he. Notice planets line up of late—let's take that for a sign.

Who's the one nearest and next? Head of an ox or a cow? Chicken's feet?
Yours faithfully and with regards. And here for my last wishes—the pizza,
coke (full strength) and cigarettes as back in the day. (Turns out the filters
are worse for you!) Life always had to end, we knew. What a privilege
being is/was. A fearful thing one might butt up against the 200th line.
IMHO, it's where we are today. Is the election over yet?

You don't need to be a prophet to know
that when this cinder Earth goes out,
every phrase will be long forgotten.
Whatever wrongs remain to right,
however much better we all and it might be;
so long lives this? So long! One shuns formality,
and yet I am sincerely yours.
So say a fond hooray.

Scrumdingling

Leigh Jordan

To the shop, scrumdingling
milk buying, with Fat Poem pulling on his leash
banging on—
smashing verse, breaking lines
gulping tinfoil bells of air.
Stuffing deflated santas
into recycled cardboard boxes.
And I once was church
on a hard bum giggling
when shoosh was the mother.
And Sheila, bless her, at the shop is waiting.
Easter, opportunistic, is peeping through a curtain
eyes of chocolate spilling.

And Fat Poem has lifted his leg
is pissing now his enigmatic tweet
upon the kerbside wattle.
Simon says stop! But Fat Poem
proud anarchist, always was
won't play that game.
Fat Poem wants a permanent marker.
The shop, two blocks away
and everyone is yeah/no
laughing lollies on the floor
where once was church, Fat Poem genuflecting
—each Sunday steals one black book.

Fat Poem pissing on evergreen Holly.
Fat Poem pissing on low spreading Viola.
Reflections of night
held in the reflection of things, things of moon
and hallelujahs threadbare in purple shadows.
All is sanctified, all is granulated. In each cracked grain
all the suns sanctified again. Each rubbish bin
a colour-coded lid. Ideology. Theology.
The hierarchy of clinging things.

Mine is bigger. Mine is better. Mine go bang-bang.
Oppenheimer was a trickster. Mother, mother
I believe! And me and fat Fat Poem are at the transept
where the collective unconscious jousts with light
where empathy precedes causation,
though god snores at night
asleep in the shell of a 4x4 Toyota.

And Sheila gives me milk.
Sheila gives me wine.
Gives Fat Poem a Sheila smile.
Once a church
my thoughts a coalescence
homogenised. My children are no longer there
nor my wife, nor the serpent, nor the lap-dancer.
One is the other and the other is many, and in the one
I am unparsed , blind to all, my madness
of colostrum leaking from the teats of a tuneless moon.
Though Fat Poem sniffing, knows
that MacHeath buried Jenny Diver
under the holy McDonald's sign.
And there are blobs of death:
Chamomiles bled in Russia, Sunflowers bled in Ukraine.
by olives everywhere, waning sick-yellow through the vein.

And there is so much pain in Sheila's see-you-later smile.
Fat Poem whining, nuzzles her shin.
Fat Poem empathising, touches sad;
touches the prosodic of all the big little things.
Once was many churches
was onion weed, was daffodil. Post and meta modern.
Demanding definition, demanding a domain.
and behind us the path is a dry-rot breath
of age dancing with entities retrocausal. There goes time.
Fat Poem is off his leash. He knows, as mere observers
we dare not
look back!

Recent sightings of Tito

Jennifer Kornberger

1.
He blows into a conversation
I have with a retired
speech therapist from Munich

Back then, she says, *I wanted*
to get in my car and drive
non-stop to Tito's Yugoslavia,
he was the wind in my hair.

Her words fluster my
southern hemisphere education

I grew up with acres of ocean
and a sea breeze off the coast
of southern Queensland
that was stiff-lipped about Yugoslavia

mouthing the dun-coloured story
of a place on Earth where meagre
helpings of hot cabbage were served
by a dictator with a faintly ridiculous
name, who, un-killable, surfed history
like a professional board rider

Why, I ask her, *did you want to go there?*

She answers, *it sounded to me like freedom.*

2.
Close to the Italian border
I find Tito's head
painted in fine monochrome detail
on a semi-circular panel at the entrance
to the Tito Cultural Association of Izola

above his head like a double halo
the Slovene and the Italian names
of the art-house, with the word 'Tito'
in parenthesis

the speech marks
like rudimentary cherubim
hauling his name heavenward

his jaw is set in a cliché
but the cheeks are soft
his visage is stern and content
except for the right eye
which appears hypnotised
by an afterimage

as if it beholds in full colour
the folk of Yugoslavia
parading before their leader
in a posthumous review—

people mock or smile, one takes out
and puts back a pair of false teeth
then gnashes them at Tito

a woman bows
another bares her breast
holding her nipple to him

one sings a strident hymn
an open bible in her hands

spittle sprays onto Tito's face

many wail
and reach out
to embrace him

a thin man carries
a complete skeleton
cradled in his arms.

3.
I glimpse him several times
in Bleiburg, in the south of Austria,
arriving and departing from discussions
about the massacre there
at the end of World War Two

because this is where
my husband grew up
under a mountain
whose heart is a lead mine

a place of bi-lingual melancholy
where fields of sunflowers
bend their necks
over fields of human bones

I try to catch Tito
before he slides off
the ends of sentences

to ask him about the deal
he made with the English

ask him about the thousands
of bones which have taken root
and sprouted hatred

but he raises a hand
places it over his mouth
and turns.

4.
At a theatre performance in Ljubljana
we watch the cast slowly form a line
and begin to take off their clothes

weeping, each one gives
a personal report
on where they were and what
they were doing when they heard
that Comrade Tito had died

they are Method acting—
taking any bruised memory
and pressing it to produce
a flow of tears

but when they are scrotum naked
I see that there is no Method

they are not acting
these stages
of grief.

5.
In Stolac, Bosnia, above the wall
outside the Mehmedbasica Muslim
Guest House where we are staying
for 25 Euros a night, a small rock
rests against a brick chimney

on it a five-pointed star with 'TI'
painted to one side and 'TO'
sloping off to the other

as if someone has whispered
these two syllables as a daily charm
against hostility ever since Tito died

and people began to think
of themselves first
as Serb, Slovene or Bosnian
as Croat or Kosovan

ever since the war
gave people
the freedom to
unpeople each other

this stone mnemonic
has been placed
in the sightline of guests

as a way to survive

in a town where Muslim
memorials are now wheeled
in and out of torture sites
to avoid being smashed.

6.
Even though it is snowing
on the road to Murska Sobota

for much of the journey
our Slovenian driver
locks eyes with us
in the rear-view mirror

he is speaking about the shoe factory
he worked in when he was a 'Yugo'

tells us the employees owned the factory
describes how they walked the shoes
right into the free market, made a profit

tells us that people complained about
the length of the co-op meetings

he breaks the eye-lock

complains that he does not own
the car and there are no meetings

he drives into the whiteness
scolding the weather

scolding Tito for living so long
for dying too early.

7.
From Wikipedia to Wokipedia
to is fifteen miles
of text written
about Josip Broz Tito

when I gather the pages
and feed them into the bonfire
Tito rises in the smoke
holding a Yugoslavian passport

with its red cover, gold embossed
with six flames leaping as one
surrounded by ears of wheat
a star at the top

worth more than a U.S. passport
on the black market
when Yugoslavia was the zone
of freedom between the frozen
crossfire of East and West

you could travel to London
or Moscow, do business
in Berlin

a warless citizen.

A wind is blowing the smoke
in fitful bouts.

If my eyes are smarting
it is because
I have lost a country
that was never mine

I'm homesick for a region
on Earth that might exist

I've developed a nostalgia
for a future

somewhere in-between.

Before wind drives the smoke
into tendrils, wisps,
before it becomes
just the sulphur of someone
burning an old passport

Tito plucks the red star
of the south Slavs
and places it like a coin
under his tongue.

Sanatorium

Jakob Ziguras

I

In Autumn you decided to forgo
Italian journeys for a mountain cure
among these ruins—city air, impure,
exchanging for the poverty aglow

in stoves where elders burn raw coal or waste,
and plumes are mingled with the fragrant mist
swaddling a stanza of the Akathist.
The priest, you find out, has exquisite taste:

in youth a poet, he admired the prose
of the strict Beckett, wrote on Leśmian, Klee.
But silence calls and we must give away
all that we have, and like the watchful crows

perch in the lavishly denuded boughs—
above a brittle trash of shields and crowns—
of trees that drag their worn, embroidered gowns
through smoke, renewing their schematic vows.

II

The fridge is covered in magnetic words
when you arrive—or rather, I.
Disintegration plays on Spotify.
Shades shuffle, hoarsely, through abandoned wards.

Night spills crude oil into myriad drops.
Thus Darknes cleaved fast upon the backs
of Looking-Glasses, them illustrious makes.[1]
The window, double-glazed, whose framing crops

the starless background—see your image sink
into the shallows of the other room …
built for consumptives … Countess von Colomb
persuaded Hermann Brehmer … leaking ink

upon your grazing fingertips that swirl the tain …
pages like ants raiding a plate of crumbs …
a kitchen lamp that ominously hums …
the freshness outside—darkness, stone and rain.

[1]The lines in italics are taken from Joseph Beaumont's "Psyche."

III

A harsh light in the kitchen separates
the stacked and gleaming dishes from the rest,
remaining to be washed. An endless test,
yet one more round of suds and greasy plates—

this moment smearing like a viscous sauce,
this poem smearing it across the page—
the mind of failure one acquires with age,
trapped in the outer suburbs of the Source:

wide streets, car dealership or chicken shop,
low chainlink fences, threadbare tennis courts,
a stoner boutique full of pipes and quartz,
the hell of memory. When will it stop?

Returning through the pines, the priest you met—
paint-stained and pushing, from the Orthodox
chapel, a barrow full of trash and rocks—
revealed your heart too dry, your eyes too wet.

IV

Beside the reed-crowned pond, the autumn sun
is smoky weakness, swaddling pale yolk.
The present absence of the happy folk—
who fortunately linger at the dun

and rusting verge of vision—not by chance,
reflects gun-metal grey, the great machine.
Yet, on the fetid pond a stolen sheen
still bears the breath-prints of their breezy dance.

Here, shallows flow into exilic marsh,
or nile bend, where failed explorers gaze
upon the changeless ruin of their days.
The lead-lined sun is uniformly harsh

in its procession through the trees, incensed,
a waft of wrath, on which the light-boned birds
suspend their tintinnabulating words;
the perfect work is endlessly commenced.

V

Loss, in the early dawn, crepuscular:
brown smoke unfolding from the chimneys stacks,
dark trees that bear upon their wind-lashed backs
a lead sky punctured by a pewter star.

Night, gnawing at its stitches, bares the wound
of the horizon, bloodily bedewed.
The image is, predictably, renewed.
A festival of failure, pines festooned

with rank effluvia of poverty
that haunt their evanescent ermine stoles.
Old men awaken, don their musty roles,
recalling childhood, rusting heraldry

they shuffled through to school. Their body shrinks,
exhaling perfume like a wilting spray;
skin turns to paper, as a cursive day
is written down in blood and other inks.

VI

The mushroom pickers, watchful as flâneurs,
discern between the toxic parasols
and the flamboyant; their attention crawls
among wet needles, over roots of firs,

as glossy as a beetle, then dissolves
in misty ambience. When evening falls
the forest echoes with the urgent calls
of clashing bucks. As lean as myth, the wolves,

pad silently, patrolling their terroir;
their silver nibs of fur in cursive write
on cool, blue airmail paper, to unite
the porous pack within a single spoor.

You tap the path ahead and fear to meet—
athwart the slick ascent—a form that could,
if threatened, drench with your astonished blood
the understorey green around your feet.

VII

The smell of resin. Apodictic sun
briefly constructs a world—the potted plants
like paper cut-outs, while a young monk chants—
and then, by concrete clouds, it is undone.

Then secondary movers load antiques
(their off-white van is veiled in plastic tarps),
divans and footstools—while a poet larps
to be admitted to the wingèd cliques—

into the now abandoned cinema. The pose
assumed, a heavy curtain, may be drawn
aside to grant admittance to the dawn.
The cost of this remains translating prose.

The young Kieślowski rides a bicycle
across a postcard, framed and monochrome,
and keeps on riding infinitely home,
the reel unspooling, paradisical.

[2]The passages in italics are taken from Alexander Blok, *Poems of Sophia*, translated by Boris Jakim

VIII

A middle-aged Hans Castorp, you retreat
where rusted pines and broken statuary
backdrop the shadows, in their finery,
who take the air on antiquated feet.

Half-hearted auditing of old debates,
and tepid glances into Kirghiz eyes …
Elsewhere, another hopeless conscript dies,
almost believing that he liberates.

Refugee children playing in the snow
or drawing hopscotch courts in coloured chalk …
Walking, you think of Alexander Blok:
Praying and weeping, though wild *winds would blow* …

the snows of winter … cover everything.[2]
But snows of spring? Untimely nothingness,
blank antidora for the priest to bless;
yet in this ermine, also, kneels the King.

IX

You walk along a virid colonnade,
beneath a trembling entablature;
the scales transform to powdered wings and stir,
receiving wafts of what the forest made

in some dark clearing—redolent of sap—
in which a beehive, called by semantron,
empties to gather meadow pollen. On
the rusting leaves each footstep leaves a trap.

The morning silence hears the young priest sing.
Beneath great folded wings, as green as grass
that never withers, burdened exiles pass
to sit beneath an icon, whispering.

The trembling of repentance. Flakes of skin
fall to the tiles—desiccated nouns.
Trees start to speak in leaves, wind stirs their crowns.
Yourself the sun now hammers golden thin.

X

A spring day, thickly with a crayon daubed.
A tree, against which shadows fondly lean,
at noon, to shelter. Linger, in between.
Disfigured statues, in that absence robed,

await the ministrations of the moss
on mouldy pedestals; yet, grass surrounds
ruins and springs up from beneath all grounds—
always recovered from the snows of loss.

Remember? With a toothpick dipped in milk
you hid this once; now pages crease like skin.
The green has condescended to begin
within an amnion of bluest silk.

A lambent wind disturbs the pollen swarms,
and ruffles orders of imposing pines
so that they ring out, piercing, clear as tines.
Fragility is worshipped by the forms.

XI

The mossy armchair rock and pine create
receives your drifting, in an idle wake,
beside the body of the forest lake—
it drifts away; you count the breaths and wait.

Nearby a folly that neglect knocked up,
of stone; the flighty birds, atwitter, preen.
Naive sight paints a sentimental scene,
the clustered trees like brushes in a cup.

The onion dome shines, golden, in the pond—
where svelte ducks gather to accompany
the ritual procession: cloud and tree—
the day unfolding, tactful as a frond.

Outside another village bodies rot.
You read the Guardian. On the threshold black
sunflower seeds like teeth destroyed by lack.
Flags, scavenging, alight upon the spot.

XII

Asperged, the apples in a garden plot—
the village vacillates, becomings woods
here, at the edge, as moist, penumbral moods
beguile you, pausing by an empty lot—

inscribed by worms, hang clinging to the bowed
and mildew-powdered branches. Hard rain raps
against your beaded hood. Between the gaps, a
crystal discourse trickles; having flowed

beneath a guarded portal—flames of green
rippling on either side—it percolates
through mossy village huts, concrete estates, as
reminiscence tinctures the unseen

like blood in water, luring graceful forms from
crushing heights, and yet by modest bells made
meek. Each peal awakens broken shells, as
lightning shouts the peace beyond all storms.

Five Elegies

David Bruce Musgrave

1. In Memory of Ross Hannaford

Sixteen months before he died I saw him play
at The Red Wheelbarrow
in orange jeans and an orange silk shirt,
just a guitar and a delay,
feeding little riffs into it
until he'd hit a groove which he'd then overlay
with improvisations. In the narrow
room he seemed like a tiger caged behind sixteen repeating bars
every few minutes kicking his left leg out
as he finished a phrase or wobbled the tremolo arm,
his big black sandal almost hitting my knee
then retracting, and playing on with that goose neck bobble
I remembered from GTK
when I was six, watching Daddy Cool
play 'Eagle Rock' in a milk bar,
but instead of that plastic lifesaver's cap with a propeller on top
he wore an orange beanie to match his cool jeans.

It's funny how music is a form of time travel
which punts us into the past. I learned to dance
with the daughter of the co-founder of One Nation
(not that I knew that then,
only that Anne, with her twin sister, had just arrived
from Adelaide already knowing the steps,
elegant, sophisticated, blonde and aloof)

It was the summer of 1977, my last year of primary
and 'Eagle Rock' was the stop-start soundtrack
to learning how to lead and dosey-doe.
Later we became friends: she sang in my band,
but her sister Debbie was another matter.
Once, when we were studying *Lord of the Flies*
our teacher had us imagine a scenario
in which we were Piggy, Simon, and 'friends':
how should we not end up killing each other?
In my Dudley Do-right way I suggested
some sort of toastmasterly democracy
a benign formality, naively trusting in 'rules'
but Debbie's response was fierce, her black curls shaking:
persecution follows from organization
as night follows day: no one was going to boss her around.

There were less than twenty of us.
When we stepped out into the warm November air
of Lygon Street, Ross was there, the smoke from his rollie
dissolving into the summery dark,
waiting to thank us for coming to hear him
as if we were friends at a private party
and not itinerant strangers about to part.

2. Halfway Things

i.m. Jordie Albiston

On the outer reaches   drifting
where the summer sharpens
its pacific glare on its winnowing
currents   wavery graft of blades
strewn in prismatic deep   bladderwrack
on scripted foam   deep in blue-green
homeward   resuming lemon and lime light
of tide   dimple and furrow

*

Had you never left
you'd be just here in the middle   yep
aslant and at a remove
but time has hoovered you up   yep
up and out into the cosmos.

*

This is the good place, of grass
plumping with rain, and liquidambar
seed pods like meteors burrowed by moonworms,
pebbly clay trickling with the slow runoff,
of wind conducting the skittery chorus of leaves,
suspiring pigface and gold-tipped orb-weavers
patiently cruciform   wasps embossing the leeward hollows
of dune-bedded rocks:

there is no other place, just places,
none better than this place, where you aren't.

Halfway things. Echo and abandon,
low stratus mizzling imperfection:
out of the horizon
of mortal thoughts, light disappears
into mottled yolk, livid-veined and bluish orisons
of refracted darkness. Slab-cold
wind picks off the defenceless spume.
A temperature older than fire
that inhabits all things at their core
leans into its work, a spoor
of damaged shapes, forgetful
that today is deeper than yesterday
but still as shallow as a shimmering puddle,
weird as a truckful of dewy-eyed camels
chewing sideways as they wobble over the bridge
at Waratah Station.

*

unspeakable joy unspeakable
grief irrupts playfully prolonging
itself recalcitrant rosaceous
clouds and the sun's disappearing self,
into nights that seem more permanent now,
more like a state of affairs arrived at
and agreed to even announced as angles
of carpentry mortice of coffin-boards,
dead flowers for the dead flowering once more.

3. The Fitzroy River

i.m. KEQ

In the wet this river lashes out
across the plain, a standing wave of water
out to sea. Days darken in mudsquall
boiling around taproot lightning. Levees

churn apart, the river slaps them together
again and everything sinks into clay.
All that is born returns to country,
baby freshwater crocs, gunmetal-grey,

vast shoals of cloud swimming up from the Pilbara,
and you. The cherubin disappeared here years ago,
you said, and now less fish, but a pain in your side
that nothing could assuage. In the dry,

after a dismal wet, we camped by the river, shrunk
to a freshly washed wound. We trolled it a day,
came up empty-handed then abandoned it:
unseasonal rain-clouds wattled the sky and threatened

to bog us in. At the eleven mile dam a scree
of concrete was mixed with a broken chorus of shells
on the dark earth. Leaving, we stopped to watch
the brown water flow gently under the bridge.

You said, as if you knew, 'Just a minute,
you never know when your last time here will be.'
Two months later, gaunt as a rake, you shook
my hand for the last time: 'See you soon.' And you will.

4. Siege

i.m. MJQ

How dangerous is sentimentality? Enough.
My mother took his reticence for shyness,
the way he would retreat to drink and smoke

outside, or stand behind a door, half an eye
on us, his near relations. Influenced by my mother,
I made the same mistake. Yet he called his brother

Kerry, 'Fat Guts' and each night would cow
his mother, in her 90s, into her chair.
He was a bully, a coward. After his mother died,

he refused to leave her house, turning a gun
on the bailiff before shooting himself in the face.
Years before he'd asked if the book I gave him,

Brief Interviews with Horrible Men was a gift,
or something else. I had said it was,
but now I know that it was something else.

5. Kerosene

i.m. MEQ

You knew what it was like to return home
to gutters filled with kerosene;

to be raped with the door ajar
while your mother-in-law sat in the other room;

to have watched your daughter Joy
crawl through the legs of her uncles

while your husband inched towards the day
he would father his own grandson.

Now there is more than a continent between us
and much less. At least your ex had the decency

to blow his head off in his car, leaving you
to be whittled away by years.

A part of me is buried with you, the five year-old
tiredly trudging after his beautiful cousin

across the Bridge.

A Life of Prizes

Dan Hogan

Be the counterfeit queen of the premeditated
argot you want to see in the world / Rupture
this / Rupture that / A circle
        possessed / Know the last thing by
how close it is to the first thing / Remove
all your clothes /
                from the washing machine (sicko) /
Learn the alphabet / ABCDEFG while huffing
black mould / Feathers / make good toothpicks /
Anything can be a toothpick if you have a go / Cop
a mouthful / The best form of welfare is a
feather / Phonelight floods the holes / in your
body / Soundless and high pitched blue / Hit the
snooze button / Ten more minutes / of blissful
nowhereness / At a time when the sky has been
slapped, home is a gimmick / Mow a little lawn /
make a little love / and one day posh snorkel /
Yowza / Yowza / Yowza / Collaborate with doom /
(Doomed if you do / Doomed if you don't) /
Commission the havoc of birds
                with feathers like crowbars
                to pry open new skies / Time? /
                It stumbles / as you stick your leg
out the window of your luxury apartment / How do
you find something when you don't know what it's
called? / A crowbar bird circles overhead,
                scheming / The trillionaire class
emerges / and the biosphere collapses /
This world isn't big enough for the two
of us / (The Amazon and Amazon) / Doomsurf's
up / Hang ten, you are / an interregnum of
competing vectors /

The product and the link rot / A great variety /
Finally, you are a transactional plane, the everything
store every minute of every day / a vector possessed
by a new ruling class / Jimmie the locks /
Wait for the image to take hold /
Shouldn't be long now /
Yowza / Yowza / Yowza
If you liked this / you might also like this headache
from licking icecream too fast / 1000000000000
/ What of the muted sun inherited? / The hour
dispenses its smallest trifles to its buffest
minutes / Troubles accumulate / Bin night /
Thursday / Late night shopping / The night is but
a kitten / Meow / See also: meow / A collision in
kahoots / See the cars parked in scarce clumps /
but don't take my word for it / Check the oblong
allotments / White boxes painted on black
asphalt / Describe zero as both nothing and a
mouth / Envelopment / What is a car park if not
the reaper's shadow julienned myriad ways / So on
and so the evening arranges its droplets on
the sky's keep cup / Sip, slowly / Hands free /
Portending the spectre of an ending, enter KFC
dressed as Ronald McDonald / Be the counterfeit
queen of the premeditated argot you want to see
in the KFC / and one day a life of prizes

emptiness, nulls, *nullius*

ledgers & reckonings

Syd Daniels

>>>

of history (selectively, & clenched)

today's proverb: *the egrets*

we are taught to speak

flying themselves in turbulence

this is how

***calling un-need through day rise,* the same**

nerve-stricken town of drunkard's children

way *this place no more*

UNDERSTOOD, & in our droll

belongs to us than butterfly, bigger

OF THIS WILL BE SPOKEN,

than swallows &* big as our gasp, *belongs

an unsaid NOTHING

to the waterfall's updraft

Worland's brow is a fist, hovering

>>>

stream of chunder airward, &

& how to be more

bugles a front-row

than colonizers, how to revive

& tractor-faced, big, blonde)

this instrumentalized mountain, without

Charles Somebody (bowl-cut

turning it into fetishized

spouts across pre-mowed lawns,

themepark version of itself, how

moments after 'The Last Post'

to coax time back

mythic groundwork, &

into the presence of things, patterns

offshore, digging undeeply

chiming across the slanting

preceding The Diggers soldiering

gullies trickling tadpole, tiny crays, the

massacres across decades

butterflies' iridescent waft

the land clearances & roving

arresting deer attention, marten

of lest-we-recall

surveilling ridgelines

in cross-eyed rituals

where raccoon dogs are said to shuffle, 'how

& settled, settling enshrined

to invite these back onto their own lands'

of ANZAC Day, we the blest

I ask our farmer neighbour

morning's blaze, on the asphalt surfaces

while he drenches air

we bake in the waning

with pesticide, you can see it

hand-me-down ideas, &

instantly freed from bug static, he says

his community of yawn-headed

'eh … ?' then shoves the nozzle

bully) assembles

across a widening arc, next chemtrails spurting

bowler, classroom smoker,

through the verdant

Mr. Worland (principal), seam

clarifying moment, my question

Omeo Primary School, &

morphing into *how*

<<<

to be the good neighbour

Omeo means mountain, in aborigine …'

***to nature …* & across these villages**

don't ever forget

geriatric with cinderblock dwellings

I'm talking about my heritage here,

& their unkempt dogs, how

too right'), & he's wincing, 'mate

to be more than chime inside abyss, in these

in echoes of 'fuggin

antler-filled shadows how to find

without a permit' (the bar slurring

a syntax that avoids

but can't even do that now

the deadfall nullities of wrong language

to the old-timers' cattlemen huts

>>>

I'd love to take me kids

atop the season's waterfall,

unscrewing a poison of 'personally,

a pair of slow wings

into someone's sotted face

flexing, big as our outstretched palms,

wind-soured plains, evening rolls

the mind an adjustment

the cloven-hooved

toward hope's possibilities

at the 'Hilltop Hotel,' & across

in butterfly, an almost-there

parked utes mustering

as if some new verb, unspoken, has

<<<

landed inside the day, the heart, & now

across a form's blank fields

grasping the grass-stained air

'righto, where were we?' tracing a biro

(yes, *abvolating*)

venetian blind, shuts door, asks

as if a glint or rhizome

my room's interlocutor smirks, flicks

tilting over circlets

blood & enforcement, more, until

of prosodic wind, toward

& 'fucken [redacted],' 5 minutes

the idea of sound, as if an image

he screams, they spit '[redacted]'

of an image

OUT A TRIBAL MAN, each time

>>>

SMASHING THE MIDNIGHT

in twinkling frequencies, water

howls, 3 BRUTES

lallating over rock

structural underlay to the corridor

& the mind inside the heart begins to hear

… dickhead') but the noise is mere

itself, among trees, listening

dickheaded … arrest … community

to the wind, simplifying, nemning

bureaucrats proffer uniform zeal ('prang …

the pollen-drunk bees

the copshop, overtoned

unlevel over upper altitudes, belting through
in siren, flashing light … inside

green-walled fortifications
& impromptu joyride jolts to STOP
I've been passing a blade across, weeks, & the wind
the stairs to Dave's Belmont van
scent-filled as these birling insects
liquefy, I'm limbing
semitating, flightpaths
& the solid edges of propriety
as instinctual grammar, groundwork of buds
dealer's house, then to 'Rumours' club
nubbing under birdcall, & my saw
to get properly bent, car to Bairnsdale
hits the rock, pure aporia,
whatever we can find
while a new family of deer skits, baying
to get serious & we're doing

into a matrix of placeholders, &
of wet oblivion, by dusk it is time
amid these resonances (down tools) my shadow
Dave & me staring into the nighs
blinks, recalling the gunshot afternoons
but hit the pub, by noon
of East Gippsland, silences ringing
24 hours & nothing to do
around teenaged stumbling, unken
it's a perfect day in Lakes Entrance,
on Gunai/Kurnai (ˈgʌnaɪkɜːrnaɪ) ground, rifle raised
invitation misread, &
& aiming, recreational
high school friend's wedding
through ring-barked forests, the land

<<<

wind-broken, lifeless but for rabbit

country & foreigners out

plagues, blackberry, droll blunt souls

a dull & thudding alien trope … *God's own*

of farmers dead-eyed as jailers, doing the rounds

inside mundane scenes, gabbling

checking fence lines

Arcadians threading bait live onto hooks, brutal

encircling false connection … none here, none

from these mountains, stalked by mutant

needed, as if swapping those enclosed violences

the biggest trout

for a mind, syntactical, is expressive labor or

there's pride in those who can pull

an unquiet act of will, tomorrow's proverb: *throbbing*

>>>

reckonings & ledgers

nullius, nulls, **emptiness**

Haiku Variations

Asiel Adan Sanchez

i.

blue gum at dusk
a poem in each leaf

read as they fall

ii.

boys
on the
murray

the sky
so blue
& open

spring
blessed
spring

iii.

lights rippling
across the surface

your back
the river

iv.

knowing ourselves whole
masculine & feminine
full as the white moon

v.

yarra   trams   gentle   spring

river   flowing   autumn   rain

vi.

red sun   reflects   warm soil

vii.

this land
always
is

in the interest of clarity

Christine Fontana

to: j.christ@gmail.com, jesus.christ@gmail.com, jesus.the.saviour@gmail.com, jchrist@gmail.com, jesussaviour@gmail.com, jesusthesaviour@gmail.com, jesus.of.nazareth@gmail.com, jesusofnazareth@gmail.com, jesuslambofgod@gmail.com, jesus.the.lamb.of.god@gmail.com, jesuschrist@gmail.com, jesus.h.christ@gmail.com, JESUS.H.CHRIST@gmail.com, j.lambofgod@gmail.com, JEEZUZ.H@gmail.com, christ.the.saviour@gmail.com, j.christ.son.of.god@gmail.com, jesus.christ.son.of.god@gmail.com, jesus.son.of.god@gmail.com
re: my last missive

it's not that I was expecting a reply, but. in the interest of clarity. if you had been a little less parabolic. if you had sought literary guidance. as it had behoven you, like the rest of us. if an editor had at least gone in retrospectively. if evils were in fact made weevils. then it might have been a better known fact. if people today bothered to read their histories. if you were to have held sacred the holy flour bins. had your rigidities made room for soft geometries. and if the lives of women had. if the voices of men hadn't. but mostly, if the art hadn't been so beautiful. [if the art!]

to: holy.jesus@gmail.com, jesus.holy@gmail.com, holyjesus@gmail.com, jesussonofgod@gmail.com, jesuschristsonofgod@gmail.com, jesussonofTheFather@gmail.com, jesus.son.of.the.father@gmail.com, jesus.son.of.The.Father@gmail.com, jesus.son.of.a.gun@gmail.com, jesus.son.of.a@gmail.com, jeez.louise@gmail.com, jesus.fucking.christ@gmail.com, my.friend.in.jesus@gmail.com, jesus.the.blessed@gmail.com, lamb.of.god@gmail.com, lambofgod@gmail.com
re: my last missive

i apologise for suggesting, but if your sister had been nicer to you as a child. if parental figures had been more firm. your errant behaviours. as if crucifixion. as if it wasn't. but if adolf hadn't found those justifications burning. between your lines. it's a well known fact that. if believed to be inferior. beginning with the sadducees. beginning with women. that the susurrus might have been worshiped for what it was. everybody would have known a word is only a word. if fear hadn't made their testicles shrink. we're lucky sigmund understood. if only you were. here to see that freud had your number. we might not have eaten all that chicken. well anyway, freud had your number.

to: jesus.the.prophet@gmail.com. the.prophet.jesus@gmail.com, lord.jesus@gmail.com, the.good.lord.jesus@gmail.com, jesus.emmanuel@gmail.com, emmanual@gmail.com, the.lord.emmanuel@gmail.com, IESVS@gmail.com, jesu@gmail.com, jesum@gmail.com, christus@gmail.com
re: my last missive

if the art hadn't.

[if *only*.]

to: jesus.the.messiah@gmail.com, the.messiah@gmail.com, messiah@gmail.com, jesus.the.master@gmail.com, christ.the.master@gmail.com, dei.filius@gmail.com, jesus.christ.the.master@gmail.com, jesusthemaster@gmail.com, divi.filius@gmail.com, jesusmymaster@gmail.com, jesus.my.master@gmail.com, joy.of.man@gmail.com, mercifuljesus@gmail.com, merciful.jesus@gmail.com, jesus.lord.of.mercy@gmail.com, mercifulchrist@gmail.com, merciful.christ@gmail.com, christ.lord.of.mercy@gmail.com
re: my last missive

at a bare minimum, if you could just get over the whole sex thing. it. would have saved a lot of trouble. if st augustine had had more magnesium in his diet. if by lamb you had not meant ram. and had not st jerome been so lacking. in vitamin d. had we not been told to store our virtue between our legs. and other strange geographies. and that thing you're so afraid of. nature's checks and balances. had you at least considered. if maybe venereal disease was the more effective deterrent.

to: blessed.jesus@gmail.com, blessed.jesus.christ@gmail.com, jesus.the.blessed@gmail.com, son.of.the.blessed@gmail.com, holyblessedmoly@gmail.com, jesus.son.of.the.blessed@gmail.com, jesus.lord.on.high@gmail.com, jesus.son.of.the.virgin@gmail.com, jesus.son.of.david@gmail.com, jesus.son.of.evolving.apes@gmail.com, jesus.christ.our.lord@gmail.com re: my last missive

if you permit me to repeat. on the understanding that my people surrendered our stories too easily. if you hadn't been more manipulative than persuasive. if they had had the foresight to write shit down. and your people committing such subsumptions. if your ilk had been able to control their dicks for five long minutes. if mine hadn't been such suckers. for a rollicking good tale. perhaps if less critical thinkers hadn't quite shit themselves. perhaps if you had waited for humans to evolve a bit more. before you spake. perhaps if for once and for all. but mostly. if the relics had survived for long enough to provide. if the pope had sent those DNA samples out. to be tested. if weevils hadn't gotten into the milk.

to: jesuschristourlord@gmail.com, christourlord@gmail.com,
christ.eternal@gmail.com, eternalchrist@gmail.com,
jesus.the.shepherd@gmail.com, light.of.the.world@gmail.com,
jesus.light.of.the.world@gmail.com, rabbouni@gmail.com,
christ.almighty@gmail.com, christalmighty@gmail.com,
jesus.the.bread.of.life@gmail.com, jesus.holy.sandwich@gmail.com
re: my last missive

mostly though, if your version of peace hadn't cost so much violence. if the misogyny wasn't being glossed over by contemporary. if your academia wasn't. at straws. if I hadn't been so mesmerised as a child. by the words and the words and the words.

to: jesus.the.carpenter@gmail.com, jesusprinceofpeace@gmail.com,
jesus.prince.of.peace@gmail.com, jesus.holy.redeemer@gmail.com,
jesusofvirginborn@gmail.com, jesus.of.virgin.born@gmail.com,
jesus.be.kind.to.your.mother@gmail.com, jesus.the.servant@gmail.com,
christ.redeemer@gmail.com, holy.redeemer@gmail.com
re: my last missive

furthermore relating. as to what I said about the anthropological expanse. if the smart ones hadn't been burnt alive. it's just that some damage can't be undone. and on the notion of crimes towards humanity. more especially crimes against animals. which wasn't really your bag of fish, but you didn't exactly. and by the way about that bag of fish.

to: christ.the.everlasting@gmail.com, everlasting.father@gmail.com, everlastingfather@gmail.com, lordchristeverlasting@gmail.com, lord.christ@gmail.com, lordchrist@gmail.com, jesus.wine.maker@gmail.com, jesusforgotthecheese@gmail.com
re: my last missive

regarding my last missive, if you could just take a moment to explain. if they did not speak your words then why did you not arrange a. holy erasure. i wonder if it isn't the church fathers to whom I should direct the complaint. if perhaps I would have better luck reaching you on instagram. if you could please forward this to the correct authority. and so on and so forth. and onward xtian soldiers.

Hard Work

Shelley Wylie

I

I have this poem,
this story to tell
how you hear it
will depend
entirely
on you

and the way you
know the world to be.

II

I was sixteen and
I was finally allowed
to go to a supervised
house party.

III

It was definitely
not supervised.

IV

Two dresses were purchased,
the first I wore
as I left my father's house.
The second dress,
hidden in my bag.

V

Hindsight is
a tatty photo—
a hiccup of cleavage
that was all it was
cut above the knee
showing
netball bruises
and school sock
tan.

VI

The party
a sheep farm outside of town.

The main house
the sheds
the shearer's quarters
over there
a fireplace and chimney
standing gaunt.

VII

See it as a Cluedo board
a series of spaces
passages between
weapons in plain sight.

VIII

Here are the rules,
if you don't know them

stools are better than
deep couches,
keep on eye on each other,
avoid the older
brothers
the ones who
invited themselves.

IX

This story
is going exactly
where you think
it's going, btw,
if life has taught you
where stories like this go.
It's just the details
that change.

X

In the kitchen
two boys block the walkway
with dancing.

Herded into single file
girls take turns
running a gauntlet
of semi-erections.

XI

You understand what I mean,
about the Cluedo board?
Because it goes on like this.

XII

Sean on the balcony
with a wayward digit.
William on the staircase
an invasive species.
James from my PE class
dry rubbing himself
making eye contact,
confident in his methods.

XIII

It sounds horrible now,
but I was a teenage girl
at her first party
and the bar is set
so horribly low
it's a sewerage line.

This can be nirvana
if you don't mind the stink.

XIV

I start talking with Derek,
who works at McDonalds with me.
Derek is funny,
funny like
locking girls
in the cool room
until their nipples
peak through.

He wants to show me
something

skirt over barb wire
he leads me on a loose lead
to the woolshed.

XV

Immediately
he begins to undress
cock in hand
he prompts
what are you
waiting for?

XVI

He sheds his pant legs,
remains shirted
swings for a kiss
lands chapstick thirsty lips
across my cheek

it's enough
the instinct is there,
I push and he falls
bare arsed onto
lanolin greased timber boards
his cock upright waving
like a javelin on impact.

XVII

It's funny now
this story,
it's a surefire bonding
experience.

XVIII

It occurs to Derek
that something is off,
thighs are not unfolding
like he expected

He can't be certain
but this girl might be a virgin
which is annoying
it's a task,
to be a girl's first fuck.
Gotta be gentle, you know,
gets messy.

XIX

Jim Beam lust or not
Derek has never
gone out of his way
for anything.

XX

He'll remember me
try again in a year's time
behind the hockey field canteen

when he thinks
the hard work
has already been done.

Abstract Silence [a]

Aleph

flat pack 3D poetry

NEWCASTLE POETRY PRIZE 2022

Title | **Abstract Silence** [a]

Genre |Paradox

Instructions for 3D view

1	See poem	[a]
2	See poem	[c]
3	Enjoy invisible poem	**[B]**

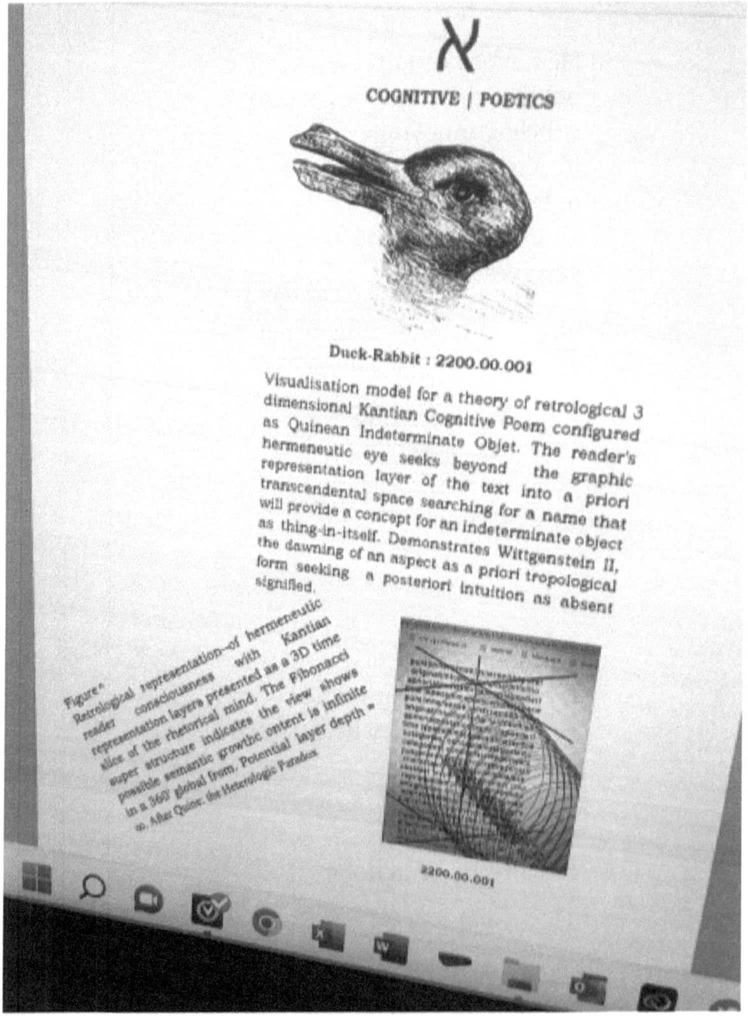

2200.00.001 Screen shot with digital thumbprint: JL Borges

Abstract Silence [c]

Aleph

flat pack 3D poetry

NEWCASTLE POETRY PRIZE 2022

Title | **Abstract Silence** [c]

Genre |Paradox

Instructions for 3D view

1	See poem	[a]
2	See poem	[c]
3	Enjoy invisible poem	**[B]**

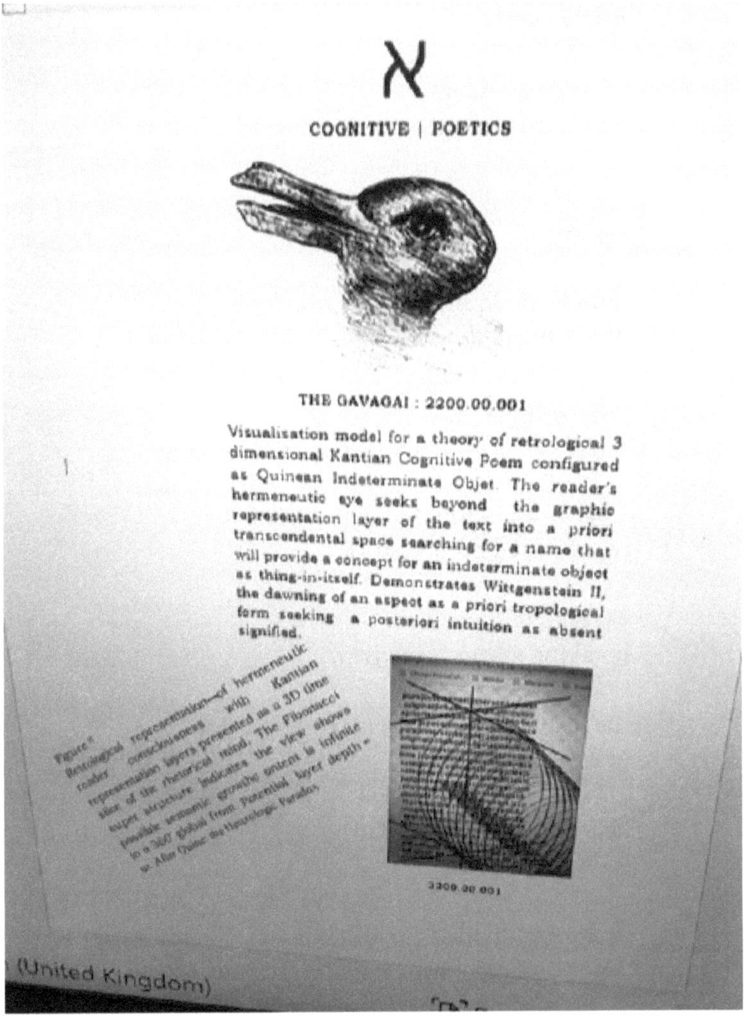

\# 2200.00.001 Screen shot with digital thumbprint: JL Borges

Gimbay Wanggal (Friendship Dance)

Nicole Smede

Gathang interpretations guided from A Grammar and Dictionary of Gathang: the language of the Birrbay, Guringay and Warrimay by Amanda Lissarrague.

In meeting
nyiirun gatha

cross deep waters
bambi divided range and valley

foot before *djina*
we weave

muscle, bone and joint in *yawutung*
preparing *guthi wangga wanyimbuwanyimbu*

hand offered
in *matjarr*

a balanced union
wipes *dhunggil* in gesture

ear held to *binagan*
breaking silence, we *ngarra*

the resonant call placing weighted step
in entrusted motion

heart beating with *yukul*
we move, in desire

no longer divided
now in graceful *wanggal wanyimbuwanyimbu*

English

In meeting
we become

cross deep waters
marry divided range and valley

foot before foot
we weave

muscle, bone and joint in journey
preparing to dance a song memorial

hand offered
in hand

a balanced union
wipes tears in gesture

ear held to ear
breaking silence, we tune

the resonant call placing weighted step
in entrusted motion

heart beating with heart
we move, in desire

no longer divided
now in graceful dance memorial.

Rain Lillies

Kerry Greer

I.

The problem was,
I could never say no to him, not
out of motherly concern or
a sense of duty. Certainly

those were there, but only in
a dormant sense, kicking in
late like a door coming off its hinges
in a storm. No,

I could never say no to him
for a different reason.

Have you ever seen flowers—
rain lilies, for example—
come back to life after
almost-death?

Have you seen the owner of the flowers—
a neighbour, perhaps—
in the garden on warm evenings,
water falling from a mint-green
watering can across the soil.
And he is pleased. He has had
a long day, and now
he breathes. There is the sky,
he says, without opening his mouth.

The flowers never turn their faces
away from him. Always they are looking
up. Waiting.

Through the window, later,
the man is visible, pressing
a crease into grey slacks.
The lights go out. The lilies

are as close and as far
from the window as they
will ever be.

Days pass, half-light hits
the tinted glass, reflecting back
the outside world, scudding cloud
and something darker than blue,
which is the sky looking
at itself.

Every leaf in the garden might
have blown to the corners
against the fence.
But the rain lilies
are very still, almost somehow
taller. Watching.

So my son was unwell.
So he was almost better.
So he said—
Mommy, can I sleep next to you?
Can I have an extra day at home?

What do the specifics matter?
I let everything fall apart
because I liked to be near him,
to watch his face watching the sky
after long days inside, unwell,
the curtains drawn.

A moon, a sun, a thimble of
light moving back and forth, ceaseless,
sharp as the axis of Death
on which Life spins, turns, catches
glimpses of its eternal shape
in lovely, smaller things, repeated—
days, or children, or the softest word:
yes,
yes, that will be ok,
my darling.

II.

Once I almost died.
I saw the moment moving past me like a white cloud
sucked into a storm. Yes, I might go too.

My husband burned alive. I want to tell you this. This is the hinge
giving way. What he did and I'll never know—
did he really want that, so much more than us?

But I only watched the cloud pass,
and when I opened my eyes,
my child was there. His child.
This boy so like him.
Except for his eyes, which are
the colour of the sky

holding everything.

I could wake every day
to him, to his vast needs
framed in simple terms.
An extra day together—
wasn't that just life?
Just day after day after day?

How could I say no?
Let the rest fall away as
rain. I was nobody's wife—
I was only his mother.
I might stretch forever
when
he looked back at me.

Commission Home

Kevin Smith

IT WAS ON the outskirts of town, a Housing Commission
    estate; everything done on the cheap, walls
so thin we could hear my sisters breathing in

Their sleep. Beyond a fence, a common, a dam
    we trawled for yabbies with bits of meat on string
we'd chuck into liquid mud. And wait. A tug

And we'd drag them across the greasy floor of the dam.
    They didn't know how to let go. Claws flexed back,
they clattered in a paint tin, ready to cinch our fingers

Lifting them out. But our reach was long beyond
    a world we had no power in. Piddling gods
of justice, we dropped them into hot water,

Just like we'd done to one another. They turned
    orange in an instant. At Christmas, my love and I,
we drive back in time so I could see

What decades had done on Hudson Street. Neglect
    was there to greet us. So too, a lank-haired couple,
standing in their yard smoking barefoot in weeds

That grew through the rusted baseplate of a mower. Broken
    cars—chocked on blocks—clogged the driveways,
fences fallen and forgotten. And there, our old

House, both front windows cracked. Cardboard
kept the sunlight out, the shame within.
Busted fibro fell into what was once

A garden my mother had tended, bruised and battered
by front-yard cricket. When I get out you stay
in the car. Next door, a port-coloured plum that's never

Fruited wears a wide skirt of broken
branches. A breeze at my feet speaks of the black
and tan terrier we used to have, run over

In front of the house. His name I forget, and where
we buried him. I lift a mailbox, its face in dirt,
and open the lid. The street is quiet. What on earth

Am I looking for? The backyard gate—a lazy eyelid—
swings from a single hinge. The Hills Hoist gone.
My father used to hang the sheep's carcass

From it, to bleed them out. He butchered them on
a chopping block. Once he turned and the carcass
was gone, my mother having swung the line

To hang the washing. Chickens lost their heads
on that block. They flapped and scrabbled about the yard
spraying with blood the grass, not yet realizing

They were dead. I imagine my sister on the porch, smoking,
finding again our father slumped in the back
of his car. It's an old story—a drunken fall

And death followed. The house has been abandoned,
a wife left behind after years of broken promises,
her beauty, her youth, lost to time and abuse.

How many doors had she walked into? Poverty,
too, an old story I learned by heart.
Care ran from here years ago and never

Came back. On Hudson Street, my younger self
sought an ounce of solace he never found.
You call from the car. I look around and I wonder

What you think of this. Of me. The air
is rancid with memories come home to roost. Emptiness
is everywhere, hope deceased, and time feeds on

Her corpse. Towering over me, a power pole.
Where the light, I wonder. I stare into silence.
Silence stares back. My love points to roses

Growing in a pile of broken rock. I snitch
two blooms the colour of blood a thorn draws
as payment from my thumb. Something moves

Behind a window. I wait; it could be me.
A wind among the weeds, a steel-grey sky
hangs over me like a guillotine. So many selves

Rushing out from underneath it. You put
the roses on the dash and we drive away. Smoke
rises into that couple's eyes; they barely

Notice it. I wonder if they'd been watching all
this time. What's in the rearview mirror is never
far behind. I raise a hand to them.

READY?

Greg McLaren

1.

Sudden hail on the ridge from clouds tinged green.
The west's fertility has slipped away—heedless
at the edge. Steep lightning slashes at the creek,
it piles thunder down in spiraling steps.
Treasury's desolate—revenue's tame flocks
topple from the precipice like venture capital.
We drank the good bubbly until the very moment
the landscape drew right in and could no longer look away.

2.

Hazardous Surf Warning passing through Auburn.
Morning rail-side: a currawong's impression of a crow.
Fight the fascists with memes. Right.
The stink and stain of burnt rubber on the footpath
means you won't want to look too close.
Sydney was Logan's Run for buildings.
Burnt branch quivers in the rain—wasn't a black bird just there?
Each night takes small nips from the last plums.

3.

The winds have kicked in now, from the east then
the west, the whole sleek season of them
heaving the grit between things, their quiet
stinging whisper from smothered highways, from sky-
dragged farms. Remember how nothing was
done but for those blubbering announcements,
the smirk-etched faces already so
deliberate and hard against any ready cure.

4.

The fever ripples out hard to a chill.
Gust follows gust in the tide-bearing trees.
Spinebills stutter and flash through the understorey.
Those lorikeets pinch time together in the wattle.
I read Bill Porter on the gold quarantine couch,
making my own strained and threadbare versions.
The window pulses in the bleak sun's wind.
Everything left to read. How will I make it to spring?

5.

Shorebirds pick around at the park's edges.
The ocean's a heavy restless blade,
but the river mooches around on its wide flats.
There is a vast mess, roiling about
in the shallow depths of the Party. Dusk
comes, you're walking now to the safe house.
I watch, follow half a moment, keep
looking as the corner swallows you, and turn away.

6.

That black ibis dipping into the kitsch cherub fountain
behind the front yard's half-enclosed hedge.
The side street pots of knife-edged pandanus,
the relict odours at the rear of restaurants. That muffled
streetlight's flicker and slur, a lousy strobe. The arcade
filled with home-printed selfies, with shrivelled candles,
kept that way, after. The state's on fire but the miners
flourish, slurping up the nectar and lerps.

7.

That year, the fires in the endless hills—smoke
from the pelts and forests and bones carries out
on the skittish wind. Birds crowd in to refuges
where the bush hasn't burnt yet, or lately,
seeking out water, defending the plant-
stashed nectar. We leave out water and seed,
slices of fruit, feel our small compact feelings
rise and pass as we watch them feed.

8.

Carrying his limp son in the rain—
Burwood Road, wet Friday, coughing facemasks
looking on under the ibis-heavy palms.
The rain stamps down, the sour sea's smell rises from the slick tar.
This wind, now across the concreted creek-bed,
flows on. *History will be kind to me because*
I intend to write it—tattooed
into the brown skin of the back of her neck.

9.

The grid drops out in a thousand suburbs.
The late urban renewal paving
shifts under my feet, a swaying world.
Obeisance to the moths and flies
at your mouth and your eyes.
Graffiti's warning glistens red, purple, blue,
in the curve of the skate park ramp—
READY? READY? READY?

10.

Grasses translucent like speared-in strands of the smoky sky.
Swallows peel up, twist whirlpool and plummet in through
the thick fuzz of bugs from the tearing front, swirling like
charred gum leaves stacked in the wind and slid to the city's
tutting back yards—grey falcons and black-shouldered kites
blur hard into them, tearing their guts as they go. That boat
by the side of the road—its wood panelling went first, curling a wedge
of thin brown then a sharply flapping red, hardly a noise at all, it seemed.

11.
Park the car nose-out in the driveway,
inch bag packed in the boot. Think I'll get out
of town. Mist's bright morning runnels
down clefts in slopes—they'll outlast
anyone's hopes and fears. The light changes,
the ridges fall dull. Bell miners measure out thousands
of paces. Wind below gusts and stills, like the traffic
stalled half-way down Lapstone Hill's terraced rise.

12.
Mist suspended in streetlights like a sneeze.
I shouldn't've left my wet suitcase back there—
bursting now with mould's bright stinking arrays.
Half a kilometre of Manildra freight cars.
one of them inscribed with a bright yellow FLASH.
I still, you know, I still. I still hear her voice.
Skull t-shirts are back in business. Ask
the wrong question, I'll have to tell the truth.

13.
I expected sand drifts' slow rolling
into those short-named towns in the west—
instead, in the city, across the flat
cold bright sun-drenched suburbs, the languid
rotting roadkill, the riffled sniff of fur
of dogs. Jackets whip up hard in the bony wind.
In my bung left ear, constant
jingling of chains or a fence.

14.
Night before noon. The food's gone off.
Snowing ash from the hacking cough of flames.
Send the kids and soft zebra onto the river
in the blow-up pool, try to hold on, try to splash out
these flaring embers. Then, walking out on the still-warm tarmac,
through the smouldering trees, past the blank blackened signs,
carrying someone's child, who has heatstroke,
across the crackling mudflats to the bridge out.

15.
We take turns to rock the cradle and weep.
This thunder rolls on in, scrolls down through
its long deep frequencies, jams its hard
light in between cracks in the dark corner.
The fraying house, the walls' slow lichen.
The sound's barrier crackles apart, knocks loose
something brittle in the wall cavity. They used
to bury cats under doorways, didn't they? For luck?

16.
Don't think I'd ever prayed, because, well,
what to? The two of you were supposed to wait
by the side door, unobtrusive, and wait.
Remember that first day, above the harbour?
And go out through the gap in darkening wisteria,
the morning glory. Wait until they go,
chasing the shouts from the front. Go. That
August night, checking the test? Remember? Go. Don't wait.

All Week the Early Skies

Mark Tredinnick

For My Parents on their Sixtieth Wedding Anniversary

1. All week the early skies of May replete
With the murmuration of starlings. A synchrony
Of acrobats in bling and black rehearsed
Against the autumn blue, an improvised
Symphonic dance applauding its own performance
Of all that could not possibly be in the every-
Day world, but is—the Beloved, who, in all
Our living too fast and thinking too hard we often
Neglect to be.
One morning as I drove
The last stretch up and over Catherine Hill,
Two troupes of these vernacular birds essayed
This one ecstatic feat, this daily dance,
Together—now beside, now behind, now before, now below,
Remembering their thousand separate selves,
Each in the other's company, the better to make
One hearth again, which, as I crested the hill,
They did, as if they'd never left it.

2. Thinking,
As I was that day of my parents' sixty years
Together, it struck me, here was a moving image
Of how you get that done. There is accounting
In it, a finely calibrated, deftly
Renegotiated guesswork, recip-
Rocal accommodation managed on the
Fly; there is a music in it, composed
As it is played. There's art in it and graft;
There's space in it and grief, but just enough;
There's grace in it, belief; there's yield; there's trust.
And I believe the gods may lend a hand
In it, the angels lend a wing.

But weather
Is what it looks like, the come and go of clouds:
A northern lights in black and white, a flame
Of shade, a shadow play of fire no doubt
Can douse.

3. I've heard it murmured among the birds
And trees good marriages are made in threes. The steady
Ones among us, the ones who see the other's
Changes out, marry three times the one
They married first. We're lovers, and then we're parents,
And then we're friends. As if to prove that rule
My mother lost her diamond twice—got it,
And lost it, and found it, and lost it, and found it again.
That's the kind of luck that starts to look like
Fate. A love, though earned, that starts to feel
Ordained.
4. Considering at my desk the other
Day all the several episodes
And increments in which some others' romances
Are made, the sheoaks that sing my solitude
Ringing the one-note carillon of the miner
Birds, I thought of the liquidambar that stands,
As if standing were a samba stalled for winter,
Beside my house. And I thought that what it takes
To thrive through sixty years is what my parents
In their cleaving teach and what all trees
In their patient practice preach. Don't stop,
No matter what. Forget the forest, don't run
The mill, and let the future fashion a garden
At your feet.

5. At Wedderburn, beside
The yellow schoolhouse, where I sometimes go
To work, two eucalypts, a pair of yellow
Box, melliodora, which blossom bees
And scent the afternoon with butter and honey,
Have stood for sixty years and leaned their separate
Ways to open a wider canopy above them
Both. And as I stood and looked at them,
Thinking the obvious thought, one whipbird
From the geebung scrub unfurled its bracken
Lash of song. And from the saplings, almost
As an afterthought, its mate piped
Its tuplet of response: nature seems
To want its circles round.
Between the trees
A bench, once nailed there, I guess, to seat
The kids at lunch, has grown the trunks around
Its ends and colour-matched their weathered grey,
And now it seems to bind the two as one.
From one of them a spinebill slides its descant
Down: if jackhammers could play the flute,
This is how they'd sound. And from the thinning
Leaves of the second tree, the older one,
A second trilling comes. For nature wants
Its name said twice: two prosper best as one.

Goodbye Look

John Hawke

Here I am, on the roof of the abandoned library,
over grimoires of Boehme, gallons of urine
boiled for a dim phosphorescence, where
complete success commingles with dismal failure:
fist-impacted plaster masked with the imposture
of a child's framed picture. Smells like magnets
never in my word land: the field of blood
and bone, anointed in late winter, crossed
in a calm time. Startled by the grey on grey
of an owl's apparition and backwards gaze,
contemplating retirement, or reincarnation
as a god of great abundance. Let me
colour in your heart. The yarrow stalks spill
like needles of starlight over creek-stones,
scattered through narrow rapids. Our happiness
will have no history: grassfire wanders
the mountain. Fall into lava and you lose
your skirt, then the poisoner vanishes
like the illusion of hairs on the moon's
clean shaven cheek. A curtain shudders
within its crush of glitter, speculating sunrise
on a day in which neither you nor I existed:
no corridors of traffic commence their vibrations,
the columns of smoke retreat into charcoal.
Only asteroids of insomnia, parallel and rigid,
with no dream pictures to cling to in the sleep
of disbelief, the myriad forms of spilled religion,
then aether of amethyst in dissolving haze.
The hypnagogic wasp of 4am, ideated
yet tangibly real enough to be fumigated,
the savage civilized, its golden signal

scaling to black noise, cobwebbed like the
dewlapped strands of human skin
wreathing a silent form stretched prone
on the footpath outside Chemist Warehouse.
I'm on a roll, says Sisyphus, collapsing over
the lifetimes of several cats: the body
honoured in every antenna of cell-walls
or discarded as refuse. That downpour
overlooked a moment ago has already
swollen and tanned the creek, tormented
with red, glanced in the swift inadvertence
of versicoloured parrots, the trance of
Butoh theatre sports with a three-year-old
drawing a line in the grass with this heavy iron
gate which must be closed, selected before
combining to enounce Les Rallizes Dénudés,
revealing a numberless number in queasy time.
Skin-tone as an indicator of unnamable malady,
viewed through migraine blank as white moon,
or a cold that cascades like shattering glass.
And when I looked, wrenched around like this,
inside the window, you were no longer there:
only a figure with its head aflame, and a man
in black, another in green, a butcher in red,
and I was just a log for your blazing pyre,
hollowed by the swoon of summer wind,
waiting to fall in love, the sandstone column
and library steps abrasive as the smoke from
an unfamiliar cigarette. Wild roses planted
in the coppered nail-holes of sheeted tin.
This authority's appearance of omniscience
is only pretense, our concealment a rift for
the sabotage of autonomy, scattering the
wavelengths of violet and blue to radiate
this sunset bleed, before the mortar congeals,
hopelessly helpless. Just doing our own thing

until I discern your lineaments through persistent
vision, the silhouette of a ghost impression
imprinted in the naphtha flare of Greek fire,
an optogram of isolate and slender flame.
And, looking back, it was never a good idea:
desire drawn by accidents of propinquity,
negative capability, or crush of shyness.
How broken love dreams about language,
leaving me abandoned, a total stranger,
except for the imaginary king in the forest
of destitute and prostrate blackwood.
Now in the triumph of a kitchen garden,
tracking a path through placid duckweed,
fully versed in the modern style of words
that barely belong together, like marriage
with an elemental spirit, tapping these
metrical rhythms in mid-air, the beauty of
the devil of youth churned out in vacuous
delirium, as lemon-cheeked cockatoos
dabble black feathers in the gilding pool,
and fiat money is withdrawn from circulation
as taxes to keep inflation under control.
Doing nothing is the best thing, then perhaps
something, but never nothing again: chance
languishes at the offer of insignificant stakes,
a secret the spectacle is designed to conceal,
like the spell a single syllable might dissolve
or the evanescent tint of an expiring dolphin
as mercury shatters through a swarm of cracks,
speechless with sorrow at the instant of parting
in second youth, rejuvenescent on the wrong side
of forty, like an interruption in elongated sleep.
A garden that guards an idyll, our seal of words
screening a honeymoon kiss: blue-mouthed
and frail, steadying a basket of carnation milk
in a corridor of Maxi, elders flanked by revenant

Vikings exposing biker beards, as 'Better Things'
haunts the supermarket radio. Take the thorn from
the thicket to puncture the cushion of the throne,
speak a pure dialect of currawong, attended
by paramedics on the floor of the ginger biscuit
aisle, circulate within the shrunken circumference
of a small inflatable pool, on a lush mattress of wine,
mithering among peevish deck chairs at the Australia
Day campground, muted by leagues of booming surf,
as protracted summer expires in a quarrel of storms.
Viewed in a virgin seeming glass, this face replicates
patterns of constellations no longer your own,
a cavern with a red handprint across its cheek,
teaching a restlessness into which no images
can be drawn, the curves of smooth manatees
after long privation, bursting into moths,
like foreign memories of a time and fashion
you failed to notice: the sleep of the young
squatting on a suitcase. How ardently I missed
every day of you years before we met, an illusion
created by deficiency of psilocybin, both of us
wasted on meaning, sunstruck in passage of trance,
syllables of bindi-eye in the long paragraphs of lawn.
The slanted waterbirds are leaning to our side.
The black snake, rattled, commas pinkly in retreat.
Rivulet's percussion of stone clapped on graver stone.
Red feather levelled on green. A sky too white
for moon printed in the dewpoint chill of dawn.

the cost price of a flaming gala

Dave Drayton

A descended young inherit shrill   atoms. A
daily ordinance emends   lists A through E.
To dully change   manners dead histories I
study and trace   and ogle nihilisms here.   O
calamity!   Enshrining   lost heroes added U
-nder   lights   so a line's decorated   a hum in y

-our earliest night. Mishandled code as   NY
minutes to carry a dislodged heel,   shin, an
arm, a length decided online.   Story is as, uh,
story is – a cannonaded   delight. Heliums re
-align similar   dancers, ended, yet- Shout, oh
Shout and   engineer a lost, charmed idyl. Is

-land made as threshing or decline, you   sit
outside and dance regimes hot   shrill any
heat'll do in need. A rusty   griminess. Ad-hoc
machinery, slighter   solutions, a deed and
agreement distils   a sunny childhood. Are
some art   nihilists? Declared annoyed? Ugh

I’ll deny riots in here. Some cads and   a thug
A casehardened dimly rousing   on the list.
Douse miscellany and other   things I read
in course holstering.   Dashed detail, many
a ceremoniously   dearest hindsight. Land
emerges as   sordidly thin; a land unit echo

ardently in disguise. A motherland   chose
endemically arid onshore.   Instead thugs
cede highrise unity   room and steal lands
heeded hands   carrying soil mount a stile
and run.   Choose a digitised shelter – manly,
hidden,   hint as roomy stun. I age cell. Reads

rites: heed a moon’s aching nullity.   Dreads
a marshalled rendition   studying echoes
echoes head lists,   daunting order mainly
disarmed a   clandestine holy iron, hugest
gesture is   aerodynamic handhold, listen:
a ceded   or mouthy sheltering is an island.

Cooks River Canal — Wangal Country, 1990s

Dimitra Harvey

The Cooks River is called the River of the Goolay'yari, the Pelican Dreaming Story... [A] man fled from battle, abandoning his wife and children, which placed them in great danger. As he stepped into the middle of the [river] ... he looked down to discover he had a webbed foot ... He had been turned into a pelican as punishment for leaving his family behind.

—from the Tempe Footbridge plaque for artwork by Lucy Simpson,
'Goolay'yari (Place of the Pelican)'

Now, it's a concrete ditch—
snaking between factories, and car lots, under
highways. And down the centre

of its slabbed floor—a spine
of water rolls seaward, scaled with diesel
and runoff. On its north bank—

a strip of cycleway white as pith,
hemmed with succulents and spiny
leaved shrubs. Ibis preen, gaze

across the bank to factory walls loosed
from their roofs—the old yards
a ruck of weeds, the high tops of the pampas

tossing like manes in the wind.
On weekends
my brother and I would leave the house

at dawn, barefooted, wild
as hares, and run towards
the bike track's gate, shuttered by shadow

at the end of the street, flanked by white houses
and their gardens of staked roses. We'd pass
fig thickets, century-twisted,

she-oak groves like hauntings of rain,
weeping willows hunched over the canal's rim—
till we'd broach

this treeless stretch, and stop. Watch
the rib-gaunt horse on the opposite bank
mill paltry meters. We'd burrow into tufts

of fennel and wait for rabbits. And from
the barbed creepers scrambling against
fences, the briars and ivy twining

around fence posts—squeezing out bolts, cranking
locks—we'd sometimes glimpse
a fox, that streak of dry blood. We didn't look

for pelicans—not their huge abrupt
eyes or rubber-flipper feet. Not for crabs
angling over mudflats or beneath

the salty knots of mangrove roots. Not for banks
purpled with oysters, or copper fish flashlighting
the shallows—we didn't ask

about the river's people, who know the king tides
of loss, its tributaries of grief. We were strayed
as cats, took damage for granted. Knew only

how a man, leaving his children, sidesteps
the river: walks the canal's graffitied overpass
and is gone.

Building the Coffin

Coral Carter

Sometimes I rest my head
in my hands to feel its weight—
it is the weight of my dead father's head
when we laid him in his coffin.
I lifted his head with both hands—
it was heavy and ice-cold.

We gathered in the carport
where once he had parked, polished,
repaired and tinkered weekly—
until he forgot how to do anything.
We had a blueprint found on YouTube—
DIY coffin building.

First, we talked about wood,
decided we would go with pine.
The neighbours watched, drank beer,
played with their baby.
The empty 1.30 bus went by
in a puff of black diesel.

Together we took up the tools.
Searched online for the finest white sheets,
click and collect, to be cut and sewed,
stapled onto the regulation plastic liner.
One son compiled the Spotify playlist,
asked each one of us for the tunes
we would want to hear for all eternity—
Creedence Clearwater, Brian Eno, John Cage.

Another son with a pencil behind his ear
delivered the carpenter's horse,
helped to decipher the plans.
Granddaughter, on her knees, sanded,
another granddaughter sewed and ironed,
son-in-law, tape measure in hand,
grandson boiled the jug for tea.

We hit our fingers, scraped our knees,
sweat from our brows splashed onto the lid.
An accidental pinprick of blood
spotted the lace pillow
where his head would rest.
To finish we blackened the pine with fire,
plaited old climbing ropes into handles.

The heaviest of us
was chosen for the test run.
Shoes off, he climbed in,
folded his hands across his chest.
He looked at the sky as we carried him
three times around the garden.

Mother was quality control.
We stood aside with our end-of-day beers
as she ran her hand over the scorched pine,
stroked the liner, smoothed the pillow.
Whispered—*good.*

Bait Balls

Sara Crane

Outside the rain has come
to hug you
            at least it's something
day is a race to get home
            though
dinosaurs are long gone.

A woman   slices   soft   middles
of cucumber, like when you ween
doses
                  fake maidenhair inside
the sushi prep station reminds you
of
when you stood outside   homeroom
shaking branches
         unearthing fossil paper
girls laughed in a good way.

There are still days
                 when you walk
to beaches,   shout *whale*
to quiet coffee drinkers
run
                        to the lookout to follow
tuna chasing pods   of   dolphins
pointing out,   that birds diving

into bait balls are where sharks
will be.

Sun sinks the colour
                 of an old tree, you shook
all   those   years   ago
before
you forgot
that
                 dinosaurs were gone.

Originary

Anne M Carson

How it was to be a girl
1960s, Melbourne Australia

A boy brings the appendix they cut out
of him to school A pale inert

worm in a jar I don't know the
word obscene but it is That

a worm could grow inside you
that he would parade this piece they

cut out of him a bit that
should have stayed inside him in the

privacy of his body brought out
then showed and telled in the dirt

of the playground to anyone who
would look They flocked

I didn't want to see it but he forced
me He must have put lots of red

and black into it like the red
and black I push down into my belly

Good girls don't get angry big girls
don't take up mummy's time being

scared His red and black are gone
exploded Where did they

go? They said it could have killed him
All that is left is that wormy reminder

The body can turn on you It can make
up its own mind about how much

redness and blackness   it will take
His red and black   are gone   but mine

are still there   I add to them every day
I have to push them   back down

into the only place   I know   I take the risk.

At thirteen

1969, Melbourne

At thirteen my mother still
        plaits my hair for school.
Sometimes she yanks or the

        comb snags and ouches.
Sometimes she rushes
        lunches unmade, breakfast

a shambles. I am too old,
        she tells me, I'll have to
learn to do it myself, I

        can't be a big high school
girl and still have my mother
        braid my hair! What will

my new friends think? My
        whole body droops—I don't
care, I don't want to cease

        feeling my mother's hands.
I suppose she loves me, but
        this is the only time now

her body touches mine.

The first crack

1970 or thereabouts, Melbourne Australia

They are sent in brown paper   from the catalogue
Large format   black and white

hidden amongst other approved books
novels   by accepted age-appropriate authors

Intense curiosity   obscure shame
I have to know   I secrete it in my bedroom

to read by torchlight   The first incursion
into the good girl carapace   chipping away ever since

I know I transgress   but don't know what
The book is photo journalism of the Holocaust   I'll never

forget those images   seared into my psyche
That humans could do this to other humans   My first

encounter with evil   How can I continue?
How can adults not have been changed by it?   I owe it

to the prisoners to look   learn   My parents
want my carapace strengthened to protect me   I begin

to ratchet openings   come what may.

What the picnic taught me

Always dust and heat, sparse
eucalypt shade. Our veteran
brown tartan rug was flung over

sticks and stones on verges or
patches of scrub, confident any-
where could be made home.

Nesting anodised aluminium
travel cups unzipped from their
leather case—faded pinks and

silvers, tan and peach hues. Dad's
beer, Mum's shandy, home-made
lemon cordial for us kids. Tea

from the trusty thermos, sugar
from a yellow Bakelite pie-crust
frilled, screw-top jar. Something

sharp always prodded, flies and
mozzies always struck, dust always
insinuated into sandals, between

toes. I did not enjoy the bush, sullen
'civilised' child before what was
unfettered. I identified with the

sheep—they hadn't asked to be
there sweltering either—you could
see they preferred shade, the herd

huddled under what the straggly
stands offered—why couldn't they
see it, I pleaded in my cocoon

of anguished adolescence, hating
farmers. Years after the final family
picnic, I learnt to love birdsong—

carolling, choralling, filling my ears
with melody, my eyes with eucalypts'
pale khaki grace. Years more to feel

connection—bird, tree, sky; tree,
person, ground, all apiece. Years
again before recognising even those

scraggles of bush, dusty and derelict,
had been loved and sung over, over
millennia.

I remember him only
i.m. Frederick Joseph Geere

I
In the 1920s photo he leans towards Gran   bending
at the waist   not rigid as a pole   as photos

of most 1900s husbands   men   firmed in upright
masculinity   Pop doesn't stand to attention   he's not

ready to shoot like a lance into a rosy future   He looks
playful   pliant   like he could turn cartwheels

or jokes   like he's pouring   awkward affection on her
like he leans on her   as his staff

II
1912   Tunbridge Wells   He and his brother
mechanic and engineer   built and flew   one of the first

English bi-planes   flimsy canvas and strut   over mouth-agape
admirers   Their disapproving Christadelphian parents

were probably not on site   Two years on   strictness
drove   the two boys   as far from them as possible

But one month before 17-year-old Pop   immigrated for Australia
he and a mate   on a lark   borrowed a canoe

Moonlight glanced off the river   muscular tide   and wild wind
frenzied the waves   capsized the canoe   the boys

struggled to swim to shore   clothing dragged   he was helpless
to help his mate   taking in water   sinking   drowned

III
In Sydney   as a young married man   he invented
the first Aussie solar-powered fridge   He

got ripped off for his work   swung
between the maw of depression   and elation

A vague story has him despairing enough   to jump off
the back of a moving train   His breakdown

led to suspected horrors   at Callum Park
How did Gran support   four girls   and a maiden aunt?

Mum remembered him wreathed in smoke
sitting daylong   in his chair   She'd run to the shops

for his baccy and chocs   happy   to have
something   to do for him

IV
I feel no connection with most of my male ancestors
banker   soldier   Presbyterian minister

I can't imagine them leaning awkwardly towards
their wives   or inventing anything   but Fred

my mad scientist grandfather   made something
desperately needed   by his future   (our present)

I salute him   sending warm gratitude
from my generation back to his

My mother gets the patriarchy out of her

The mother has to find her identity as a woman, and from
that point she could be able to give an identity to her daughter.
Luce Irigaray

The best thing my mother did for me
was to get the cramp and the crimp of it out of her—

her self—a house filled with the debris of generations—
dolls whose heads could only nod

mouldy parcels pushed to the back of the fridge
stained aprons, eggshells, clogged and cracked sinks

bottomless baskets of giving.
She made trip after trip—carting barrowfuls

bowlfuls, boxes of rubble; the make-dos
the bite-them-downs and the swallow-them-wholes.

The scrimped and the skimpy. She chucked
all the symbols of woman who lives for man

by man, who pivots on his word, revolves around
his sun, she chucked it all in a skip.

All the bones of contention
life gnawed down to bone; bones into bin.

She shucked off rage and passivity
skins of no further interest to her

pinched-toe shoes and tottering heels
girdles, garters and stays.

All the used tissues of demurral and
placation she had no further use for.

She practised saying *no, not yet*
on my own terms, and *I will when I'm ready.*

Only then had she gone far enough, was clean
enough of the stain, to see me.

Flirting in Norwegian

Jenny Pollak

i

So the light when it came was already exhausted
and the sky lay down like a blanket
the ocean was muttering
under its breath.

Two women stopped to ask me if ants had ears.
A native bee was working its wings
hard to remain stationary.
The sea kept coming and coming,
dreaming of the moon as a terrible white casket.

Three dogs, individually,
came to visit
and sat beside me, after which everything
began glittering.

ii

So when the new wing of the Museum
of Contemporary Art
in Sydney was a new thing
my sister saw it before I did
and told me
it looked like an orca
mating a giant corgi.

iii

There was a trill.
The way sometimes
a thing reveals itself but remains hidden.
I was focused on the waves
then on the canopy of the fig
both high and low enough to screen the sun
but not the hills.
Only the rock stayed as it was.
The trill was necessary for the soul
in lieu of certainty.

iv

Because the waves with their pointy hats
were like mountains.

That.

And the cormorant from up close as it flew
past from behind. As if I were the one driving
the warm cockpit.

v

Imagine light from a star
that has subsequently died
travelling all those light years to arrive
(how many millennia that would take)
only to be disappointed by cloud cover.

vi

The sound of two herons
greeting is another hour
that passes.

(The morning like a strange dessert.)

The shadow of the bird moves faster
than the bird.

Cicadas have gone to earth and won't return
until the sun stops its love affair with Norway.

vii

There's a poet I know dreaming
in his dark bed. Composing in his sleep
one room at a time
in praise of light.

That's how it is.
One thing arrives because somewhere else
it has gone.

Morning gleams on the face
of the poet.

The late afternoon is waving her long arms.
The sun polishes the wings of a currawong
which flare   like two lamps
at the very same time the casuarinas
which all morning have been shining
go dark.

Anthology

Anthony Lawrence

Cat Stevens: Where Do the Children Play

I'll not bother trying to save face
by saying I never owned a copy
of *Tea for the Tillerman*,

Melanie's *Candles in the Rain*,
or *Tapestry*, with Carol King
lounging in a window seat

with her cats on the cover.
I have known disgrace.
In my defence, I was sentimental

and in love with a girl whose prosthetic eye
would change from electric blue
to emerald green in the sun.

'Listen,' she'd say, looking at me, or away,
'I know it's not Springsteen's *Born to Run*,
which is always on

when I come over, and I'm not suggesting
a Greek Cypriot Swedish hippie
can compete with narratives

the writer of *Thunder Road* can compose,
but I'd rather drink mulled wine,
smoke a spliff, and hear

lyrical protest
by someone who knows
what endangerment means, in a minor key.

Glen Campbell: Wichita Lineman

Michael Stipe went on record
to say, as he reclined
in a faux fur coat

in the back of a limousine,
that *Wichita Lineman*
was his favourite song,

which elevated him, to my surprise
and delight, from being the front man
of a stage of deep sleep

to a gold chariot, flown in like a god
from a machine, as in Medea,
by Euripides. And before

I come anywhere near
to inferring that Michael Stipe
is the last word

on what makes music great,
let me add, that along
with being a fine singer, Glen Campbell

knew his way around a guitar,
and when Alzheimer's
had taken the names

of his children and his partner,
when playing his Ovation Viper
twelve string, he could still

remember the words and chords
of every song,
when playing live, a man

alone, with a band
or full orchestra, out on the road,
working the lines.

Lou Reed: Perfect Day

While I like to think I can tell
a love song about people,
rather than one

that elevates heroin
over attraction, between humans,
with increased heart rate

being a common response
to the former,
and endocarditis an end result

when considering the other,
I'm still all at sea
when I hear Lou sing

about time spent feeding
animals at the zoo,
and seeing a movie, glad he's

'spent it with you.'
And despite evidence
that it's just the record of a day

with his lover, not some ill-
disguised homage
to addiction, when I play

Transformer, with its hooks
and high camp spells
from the neighbourhoods

of New York, I can't move on
from that killer line:
'I thought I was someone else, someone good.'

Iggy Pop: The Passenger

Watching *The Lincoln Lawyer,* not the movie,
with Matthew McConaughey
driving a 1986 Lincoln Town Car,

but the TV series, in which Manuel Garcia
Rulfo conducts business
in the back seat of a Lincoln Navigator,

I heard Iggy Pop's *The Passenger*
during a scene where Rulfo's driver
is taking the scenic route

along an ocean road, or it might have been
downtown LA, where,
in a live recording, Dave Alvin recounts

driving around with his late cousin Donna,
who had a 'sharp beehive' and 'wore pedal pushers,'
along Wilshire Boulevard,

and as The Passenger died out
with a scene-change,
I thought of great music scores

and road-trip ballads that turn
what's happening on the windshield
to a private viewing

of a movie on a wide screen, as with the slow
build-up of cellos
on Henryk Gorecki's *Symphony of Sorrowful Songs*,

best while driving in open country,
or in the early hours, on city roads, every light green,
playing *LA Woman*, by the Doors.

The Rolling Stones: Winter

That year, the Rolling Stones' *Winter*
was on repeat, at home and in the car.
It was August, with sacred kingfishers

painting the upper limbs of mangroves
and tree snakes like vines.
I'd drive past mounds of seagrass,

and dugongs on road signs
like aquatic Michelin Men.
I'd always wait for Mick Taylor's solo.

The way he'd bend notes up and down
the neck of his Gibson Les Paul
would ease conflicts of the heart.

You had gone to where people go
when they talk of needing *air*,
that monosyllabic euphemism for

someone else.
Bill Nighy chose Winter
as his favourite song for the BBC's

Desert Island Discs, and Lou Reed
mentioned how, when skating
in Central Park with Laurie Anderson,

Winter had come over the speakers.
That may or may not be true,
but I like to imagine him

cutting arcs in the ice to the sound
of 'The Restoration plays
have all gone round.'

Tonight, I'll listen
to *Goats Head Soup* and hear,
at the start of track four, Mick Jagger

strum an acoustic guitar
before the band comes in, clearing the ground
for Mick Taylor's solo.

Genesis: Carpet Crawl

The doctor had a strict policy
of his patients parking a street or more away
and walking to his 'rooms,' as he called them,

adding a long vibrato to the 'r'.
There were no items you'd expect to find
in a surgery: no blood-pressure pump,

stainless steel instruments or anatomy charts
on the wall … He had a three-dimensional
cardio-thoracic model, like a puzzle

for those who like games with a visceral edge,
and he kept his drugs
under sheet music in a piano stool.

We'd sit on a red leather couch
as the notes we handed over
were held to a bare bulb. To his delight,

we raised our plastic bags full of hooch
to the same globe, for scrutiny.
On our last visit, he tipped a record

from its sleeve, and lowered it
to the turntable with a reverence
I'd seen in church, at the baptismal font.

I remember how the afternoon light
shivered like a watercolour spill
on the vinyl as a song began, the stylus

skittering over scratches before
it settled into layers of metaphor
that Phil Collins nailed, years prior

to making a career out of being sentimental.
We heard the doctor was busted
trying to sell a heel of Lebanese hash

to a detective, who must have waited
expectantly, as the proffered cash
was raised, like evidence, into the light.

Princess was here

Tim Ungaro

I

I see outlines of trees through white fog
a mountain emerging in the distance
I try to make out its shapes

II

a chipped piece of wood reminds me of the colour of past
bedrooms
saw a tractor scraping the top soil
I'm searching for a lake that may no longer exist
photographed the corpse of a young kangaroo once
there's shimmering on the horizon
but it always gets away
—hanging on the edges
of words, I wonder can I make it rain so—
and the mooki overflows—
and the houses that we do not own—
flood —I just want to burrow deep inside
inundate the halls and the stores and all - the courthouse
and the cop shop—
rain, keep raining—
earth, split into two. split and turn in,
turn in.

III

[on the phone to a police officer at Gunnedah local area command]

I tell them the story in the kitchen at the table—cup in hand —imagine them in their office—I search for the words—lay my head in their lap—conjure up everything eyes closed and all confessing

like a photograph

1 2 3 - 4 5 6 7 8 9 - 10 11 12

all wound up and swinging in the sun

and officer did I tell you about the stand of trees on a hill beside a bend in the road, where a family of wedge-tailed eagles used to nest?

and officer did I tell you that sometimes in the afternoon you could see them in the sky above that hill, hovering?

and officer did I tell you about their wings stretched outward and how the wind would blow through their feathers?

And officer can you picture the colours of their plumage—the nape and hindneck reddish brown and bare skin around pinkish eye—pinkish gape?

and officer do you want to walk with me there in the afternoon?

and officer we can lay down on the soft ground together and you can stroke my hair?

[…]

After new year I drive westwards to sunsets through suburbs built over rivers over canals and ironbark and turpentine and blue gum and grey gum and round-leaved gum suburbs built over suburbs on sandstone and asbestos and wallaby grass and wallaby bones and woollybutt and soil and clay and brick pits and apricot pips and rat spit over mountains and dark skies and dark forests burnt black and bare mallee ash and dwarf pines oh cloud-land oh waterfall-land oh junkie-land oh lookout-land of what ifs and afternoon goodbyes to Sundays and somewhere from dreaming to quiet quiet quiet mediocrity

and drive all night all night crowded in loneliness crowded in my mind with the wind and the moon and the crest of the hill reflecting starlight twinkle twinkle

and drive all day on fat lands on far flung flat roads baked and cracked and stirring scattered seeds of wheat and sorghum and who knows what a sea of brown and white a sea of green and blue a sea of yellow and grey twinkling silver steel tracks and fence posts leaning back into another time and lonely chimney stacks standing waiting for someone to come back and tell them how the family sold the farm and how the farm was built up on stolen land and how stolen land can still be bought and sold and 'who knows' and 'who cares' because it's done so let's all 'move on' and let's sing a song and sing a song and sink and sin and sing for the cinders to come and all that's piling up piling high and crowding out like memories like history like time that doesn't stop and the crack that lets in the light the crack of the lightning in the late afternoon in summer all wet and purple near the old fig tree standing almost barren now surely remembering everything and knowing what is yet to come and not knowing anything at all really

I lay down in a field and wait for the sky to fall for the night to cease behind a cloud of wet for shooting stars to acquiesce.

The bones ground down the   bones   ground   down
the   bones   ground   down   the   bones
ground   down   the
bones   the   ground

[...]

I receive a packet of papers from the police in the mail with descriptions of photographs taken of my mother hanging in a tree.

I receive a catalogue of objects that were found on the sandy bank of the nearby lake where she hanged.

I receive a piece of paper typewritten, describing the near to exact position in the landscape and the near to exact time of day that her body was found.

I receive typewritten, a summary of her final letter and the words that she marked in the sand with her pointy fingers.

tree in the water of a lake
rope rubbing against the skin
body moving in the wind
words written in the sand

princess was here

IV

And here is young Ellen in the driveway at Granville with a
curly-haired pup on her knee all smiles and innocence

And here is young Ellen and Lenny pulling young Mike in a
billie-cart and Christine and Paulie too all dusty

And here is young Ellen on the headlands overlooking the
harbour blue and orange sandstone sea and sky
beaming to her love

And here is young Ellen newly wedded in white lace and
satin standing by lurid patterned wallpaper and giving
everything to the future

And here is young Ellen in a park pushing teddy-filled pram
and babe crying harsh suburban sunlight

And here is young Ellen with babes on polyester blanket
sleepy eyes swollen but contented maybe

And here is young Ellen at round-table with Dee and
squatters in gutted river bank mansion haze

And here is young Ellen in city wet and shedding heart
pounding transfigurations

And here is young Ellen streaming rainbows into night-
veins glittering glam-rock sweat

And here is young Ellen in the Territory on red dirt with
ancient twilight dreams and distance

And here is young Ellen hurling sand-paper throated curses
at karma moths lit under wild torana headlights

And here is young Ellen puffed up and standing still in
paddock under skies turned deep and sullen weeds
rolling

And here is young Ellen in White Hart closed eye Janie's
got a gun and a whiskey sing song somewhere

And here is young Ellen crossing creek beds and
spiderlings hurling dew drops for the morning
kindness of country policemen

And here is young Ellen watching rose views and airy sweet
sweet silence never ending

And here is young Ellen early morn crawling days like all
days and thinking time back all time

And here is young Ellen settling in to mid-aged sofa setting
crock-pot and open firelight crackling

And here is young Ellen folding time with new-self writing
into being

And here is young Ellen pouring self into cradling wild
eagles into loving second life

And here is young Ellen casting cards for midnight
thumbing rune stones at westward sunsetting

And here is young Ellen speaking tongues and raising
ghosts in a cave of late-nights and long-a-goes

And here is young Ellen writing letters for her etheric body
goodbye oh good boys—good bye

And here is young Ellen winding back the womb of her
mother selective mute the withholder

And here is young Ellen easing into the great body of water
raised out of dusty mother earth and liable to bouts of
disappearance

And here is young Ellen numbing senses and laying down
with Bruce Springsteen on the sandy banks of the
devanchanic plane

And here is young Ellen in her best dress with curly hair
still growing and fresh gardenias laid out for
disintegration

[…]

One more cup of coffee before I go one more cup of coffee
for I go for I go to the valley below for I go and goodnight
Irene goodnight night Irene goodnight and goodbye and
goodbye this wine this fine wine fine fine wine fine wine
fine wine fine fine wine fine wife fine wife wine fine
done done done done and dusted dusted done dust dusted
dusted dust my lub lob lobe love love love my love won't won't
you won't my love love love love my love won't you
my my won't you buy me but my lover won't you buy me a
diamond diamond diamonds diamonds please please
please please don't forget forget goodnight sweet sweet
sweet sweet rain sweet rain sweet cyprus cyprus
under viaducts all wet all wet with rain and sweet river
flowing full and starlight and sweet Irene dancing under
moonlight moon dance moon beams moon man star man
star bright bright star bright goodnight

[…]

—I'm still waiting for you to call me back.

V

[a magpie calls out to the in-between-light]

a woudou wun woo woo

---

a woudou wun woo woo boon woo͒

---

a woudou wun woo woo boon woo͒

---

a woudou wun woo woo boon woo da-dal

---

a woudou wun woo woo boon woo da-dal

---

a woudou wun woo woo boon woo͒

---

a woudou wun woo woo boon woo͒

---

a woudou wun woo woo boon woo͒

[duration 0:45]

[an emu stands in plains grass and begins to drum]

dum dum dum dum

dum dum dum dum

dum dum dum dum

dum dum dum dum

du-rrrum du-rrrum du-rrrum du-rrrum

rrrum du-rrrum rrrum du-rrrum

[duration 0:36]

[a wedge-tailed eagle flies above a paddock—it is called kaputhin, the messenger]

---

watta-ta watta-ta watta-ta watta-ta watta-ta watta-ta

watta-ta watta-ta watta-ta watta-ta watta-ta watta-ta

---

watta-ta watta-ta watta-ta watta-ta watta-ta watta-ta

watta-ta watta-ta watta-ta watta-ta watta-ta watta-ta

[duration 0:38]

[a pelican in the water, the surface is mirror-like]

---

gno𝄐 gno-gno-gno-gno-gno-gno-gno-gno gno𝄐

---

gno𝄐 gno-gno-gno-gno-gno-gno-gno-gno gno𝄐

[duration 0:31]

Intents

Anne Elvey

1

a leaf
wind

tastes
sun

whose
reckoning

shifts
like the

mite
nestling

in woody
damp

mute or
heard

2

decay

signals to
what we can be

evidence

3

the wear of
a thing

comes with
oblivion's

stealth or
memory

always un-
expected &

familiar
on the whole

4

four spells
insist

ibises riding
a thermal

a bodysurfer
catching a wave

the sought word
written

your just hope
met

5

across the glass
light late

afternoon
the cormorant

glides beneath
the cormorant

who flies the
curve of creek

you are learning
a meaning

for losses
chosen for living

how a grief
can mirror

the sail of
your becoming

6

fissures
run thready

& deep
separating

generations
deep as the

experience
of another

deep &
incommensurable

as testimony
as a telling

that slants
towards truth

7

in late
evening's

dribble &
surge

curtains stir
with sway

of weather
your pulse

vulnerable to
belly's

breath
as you witness

these undulations
of the impossible

climate again
as edge

Vertigo

John Kinsella

1.

Inner ear to inner ear,
says the brushtail possum
that won't appear to order,
indifferent to divergent
evolution as it balances
moonlight out of darkness,
as it reads against 'species'
and vocalisations. I know
its signs and it's very
aware of mine. Neither
of us are collectibles
and neither claims a ghost
of a hope of a chance over
an argument of science.
Our relationship to coating
on a corrugated roof,
to pitch and elevation,
to peak and trough
is more than arrangement
of chapters, indexes
or hypertext. Tail helps
balance in difficult moments,
a climb through light
is a play on reflectivity,
a flight beyond canopy,
deeper than that void
of a hollow; whereas,
I use my hands to steady,
flapping the *about* as if
I am falling further
than this ground, floating
out of synch and outside
our timeshare. Overhear,
oversteer adjustments,
either side of our ear-
drums, in spirited equilibrium.

2.

Each new flowering
is another step
towards disarmament.
With few objects,
the details become
retrospect. Where
am I worshipping
without hereafters.
Addicted to method,
a conference of answers.
That plenary of kookaburras
dominating passerines
on a hillside. They are
making *their* 'range'
redundant. Impossible
to unravel keratin
from colour, so sunlight
in rainclouds dissipates—
water feathers more
than blood, and predators
will know this. Collectors
for natural history museums
with their sudden bouts
of *scruples*. They will
be the last to disarm
(they have protocols!).
Caught in this vertigo,
which flowering plant
am I describing with-
out taking a sample? Pure
observation, with nothing
botanical to pin down
or press between pages.

3.

I breathe fast-slow
through vertigo,

hearing a beautiful voice
which is sadly enamoured
of guns and war machinery—
I cannot catch my regional
balance. This is where
we are and theory can
only harm us further.
Vertigo is the eclogue
if not a soul-self dialogue:
potatoes growing
from undug potatoes
will eventually let go,
at least as we have always
known them. They
were never planted
in rows, and refuse
a post-mortem. And we're
noting insect species
we can't identify—there
are more every day;
this must be a plus.
A list of minor ailments
among wanderer butterflies
is growing out of proportion.
Timescales are vulnerable—
so easily dislodged.

4.

In such modelling
I fall short; neuro-
hackles risen, exposed
on a realtor sign, back-
dropped with each passing.
What is the audience for vertigo,
sidestepping re-runs
and countering intuitives?
Pieces of resistance. Pièce de résistance?
A quality of. Moon slipping
through me incomplete
before I am able to

take on sleep, rocking
across the springs.
I can no longer speak
of selective gradients.
How far we fall before
flattening to plain.
Epochal denials of immediacy.
Onion-grass prison bars
more or less interim.
Sleeping in that crumpling
bed of nails. Dis-en-greened.
A system of co-ordinated
moving parts. Eyes taking
in too much, and ears
capsizing. Vibrations
startling possum staying
out of sight. Each day we
try to stabilise soil and rocks.
Less more, less less.

5.

A grammarian of parrots
who slips because their
gyroscope is out of kilter,
risks commas and apostrophes
in the 'displaced parrot
beak flap tear'[1] according
to MRI-arthroscopists.

I notice a slight increase
in flock sizes of ring-necked parrots
this mid-year, but their tears
still gather on the fruit-
tearing tips of their beaks.

Each observation I record
out of the meniscus
lifts hope for repair.

6.

Early nineteenth-century
        etiquettes of English grammar
        okay the use of comma
between verb and subject.

I do this when affected
        by vertigo, but it's not
        a defence of the language
structures of that period.

A gecko sleeping beneath
        loose bark might be disturbed
        when you don't intend so,
and will pause before

finding the energy to reach
        another shelter. During
        the demi-cold of 'mid-year',
why should it shed its tail from fright,

the epitome of its sleepy future.
        And so, both of us will
        alter perspective. And
the possum will growl from its gable.

[1] *See Journal of Arthroscopy Techniques, Vol 8, Issue 7, July 2019: 'The Meniscal Grammar Signs'*

Red

Larisa Jacono

I was six when I asked my mum what chink meant
spotted through our tinted car window
the letters sprayed in grunge red
on our rusty garage door

chink chink chink
in my armour

I felt the warm Banksia breeze
whisper and mourn
gold rush ghosts carried bamboo baskets
while their tents burned
spirits buried beneath filthy golden soil
unable to scream
overpowered by fanfare trumpets
and singing children

My body smelt of sweat and fear.
ironed shirt, leather shoes
neat tie, stockings, pleated skirt
English tongue, Anglo name
did not shield my slanted eyes
foreign face

the sound of footsteps thudding
menacing shadows before
        a blow in the face
stinging cool blood trickled down my pig nose
droplets,
forming a ruby pool
blonde tatted teenage boys against
a skinny Chinese girl

Go back to your country.

masked lady on the train took two steps
children copying her eyes
of contempt
the plague followed me into
the carriage
a target plastered
waiting for the archer's arrow
to land on its neck

Your people are all like this.

threw away mum's handmade dumplings
scrambled for coins to give to the canteen lady
dumped in the wrong laundry basket
a yellow stain in a sea of white
wishing to have its tinge washed away
bleached.

My friends speak to my mum
in their native language
I asked my mum why she
did not teach me her natural tongue

Because you are Australian.

I still do not believe her.

Halls Creek Road

Glenn McPherson

Heading east with the bats,
street lights whirring overhead,
I come to the rise leading down,
down past the Manilla Rivergum
Caravan Park. I stacked my bike
here last summer, attempting to ride
with no hands through a storm.
The small green flash of television
Cricket matches, the theme song
From MacGyver show up on the fake
lawn and fold up fold-up chairs, between slats
in the three steps leading
up to a screened room.
Mr Winter tilts his head to me
before pulling another drag
from his B & H Gold.
Down by Chaffey Park
it flattens out. Walking is easy.
Grasshoppers mingle about on the edge
of the road. Every now and again
one brushes my jeans or lands
on a fence post. The moon is full
and they say it's the stars,
out west, you miss. Not me,
it's the darkness, years later, I will seek.
You have two longneck bottles
in a plastic bag. I don't ask
where they came from. A short while
back we received an envelope
stuffed with cash and a note—
to the reverend …

Alongside the golf club, sand buckets
shift slightly in the wind's lift
like mysterious hammers
on a stripped-bare piano
firing to some unseen ritual.
You told me, after I won
the Apex, ANZAC prize, that
poetry and war are a crock of shit.
I remember this as we reach the gate
to the party. Inside I am lost
straight away. This is my country
but the beer is not for me.
I sit and listen to Guns N' Roses,
take a piss behind the corn
at the far end of the veggie patch
and grab a few burger ring chips.
It's the walk I like
on the way home. A young, grey horse
is tearing at the new grass
by a paddock fence. When I run
my hand along its flank, a shiver
carries the length of the earth,
down to the Namoi River,
across the weir where later
you will skinny-dip half drunk
and climb the fish trap
like its Jacob's Ladder,
and you, an angel of the Lord.

Requiem for Ronald McDonald

Damen O'Brien

McDonald's Restaurants advised there was no truth to the rumour that Ronald McDonald was dead.

Goodbye, Ronald McDonald, though I never
knew you at all, you're my Norma Jean, my JFK,
my Big Bopper and my whopper all in one. You had
it over Grimaldi, Bozo, Grock, you were cleaner than
Krusty. They've hung up your size 30 shoes, your
snazzy bows, you walk among us now as just a man
and we do not know you, like Santa Claus on holiday,
like Superman with glasses. A clown without his suit.

Now you've gone before us with your Crew,
your Gang, your Homies, your 1 Percenters: that
purple creature, Grimace, the Hamburglar, Birdie
the Early Bird and all the rest, a team assembled
to assault the Marvel Universe, more anti-heroes
than caped crusaders. Did you think when you were
auditioning for the part, that Clooney, Bale and Kilmer
were out of reach, but you could hope for Ledger?

The passing of an age is rarely marked, as yours
was missed. Your ending should have been big.
I'd have it scored by Webber, sung by Pink.
They'll say the American Empire began to fall
the day they discontinued you. America has never
gone to war with any country that has your franchise.
Let all things pass, let all the hungry sing
what tunes they may. A requiem for Ronald.

Truly this is a time of clowns. We've had our own,
propelled to victory by a whoopee cushion worth of votes.
One waits to storm the White House once again. If you
squint, he looks a lot like you. The same fast food tweets.
Our clown started out in fish and chips, but we're
all hungry for your brand of truth and justice
and can't be filled. We've all felt buyer's remorse.
We've digested the triumph of hope over experience.

So long, Ronald, though you have gone,
your legacy, your mnemonic for our time, remains.
You gave us all beef patties, special sauce,
lettuce, cheese, pickles, onions on a sesame seed bun.
We marvelled at your alchemy, your cuisine,
but have we lost your sauce forever? Are its secrets
undiscovered? Did you go to the grave still burdened
with the recipe for your magic spell unspoken?

Will you lie in state like other rulers, Kings
and Queens of men, for pilgrims to file past you?
Like the swirl of mourners for Mao or Ho Chi Min
or Lenin? Will they embalm you, so that children
can blow their noses when they see your red nose
poking from the inch-thick viewing glass,
from the golden coffin in the crypt beneath
Headquarters, shaped like a burger box?

I miss you, Ronald, so many happy meals
we shared together, so many plastic toys
that did not last the day, bent out of shape,
that never met the weight of expectations.
But such is life, an endless progression of
empty calories, wilted leaves and sugar buns.
When all that's left to console us is that
eternal ice-cream topped with anaphylaxis nuts.

When you left us, we did not know it. Where were
your wailers? The sackcloth? The 21-gun salute?
Where was the progress through the streets of a
million overweight diners, crying in their napkins?
Remember Mother Theresa? Remember Lady Di?
You deserve no less a crowd than Gandhi. He could
pull a crowd of thousands. You went without a bang.
No questions in Parliament. No Royal Commissions.
No petitions. No grass roots, grass-fed campaign.

When you were at the top, what was your secret
regimen? As we gained our tyres, our saddlebags,
you remained the same, thinner perhaps, or
sadder, maybe more crow's feet, though if there was grey

at your temples, we never noticed. Everyone deserves
their dignity and you wore those fiery wigs.
As Australia's children gained weight, and went for
burgers after Grand Final Day, you never changed.

When you were in your prime, we still
had the Amazon, we still had multinationals
with great exploitative supply chains, your
workers still earned less than minimum wages.
We all grew up together, didn't we, Ronald?
Oh, we're all still doing those things, but quieter,
shame-faced behind the pancake of our makeup.
There's less Amazon now and most of it is burning.

Did you pass under those final Golden Arches?
Will you find your eternal rest, or will you join
the other immortals? Like that burger that they say
has never aged, that patty you could chew on until
the end of days, the one that Pharaohs would be
happy to serve in their pyramids. Or that gritty
soft-serve dog extrusion that doesn't actually
contain any food, though maybe it contains the world.

I dreamed of you last night, Ronald, you seemed lost,
sitting in that icy booth at the back. Things have
changed now. You can't order at the counter,
not if you want service. It's all done with screens,
it's all online. A guy in sweaty leathers can deliver
a lukewarm burger to your house. They sold
you out long ago and kept on selling,
their business model is written in 57 tongues.

We'll all retire or be 'retired' one day. Inevitable
as death and taxes. The PR men, the focus groups
will look for something new. Buddha Bowls? Sushi
rolls? The Colonel and his seven herbs and spices
has retained only his initials. What was it for you?
Clowns have always been suspect, often feared.
before IT crawled out of a toilet and gave us all
constipation, there was something about a clown.

Is it true that clowns cry on the inside? You were
always crying in those party rooms that McDonald's
used to have. Trust me, I'm a parent, I know that
you were crying, as you fed them fists of chips.
Oh Prince of Clowns, your rest has finally come,
they've closed the play area, prised the last ones out.
Set down your coke, dab your chin, let someone else
take out the rubbish and wipe those counters down.

Oh Ronald, we weren't plotting insurrection,
we weren't Dumbledore's Army, or fifth columnists.
If a policeman stopped us in our clowning gear we could
only answer to your name, or so the stories go, but
none of them are true. No secret rituals or conventions.
Just lost boys waiting for their Peter Pan, just an abandoned
priesthood waiting for the second coming of a curly haired
messiah. Oh Ronald, I am forever in your club.

The day will come when you are just a wrapper in
the wind, a straw lodged in a dolphin's throat, when
even memory of you has faded. Let that day be yet
to come and far away. Let the long divestment of
your assets take an age, let cartel proceedings remain
far off. We'll mine the asteroids of the Oort with
greasy suits, the only food that can survive the vacuum
cold. We'll speak of legends, we'll talk of you like myth,
we'll sing this requiem for you, until you come again.

Coffins

Verity Oswin

The coffins were only props—
nevertheless it would be an expensive scene.
It turned out you couldn't rent them
and they were tricky to acquire second-hand.
The producers argued that fewer coffins,
if artfully arranged
could be equally impactful.
The director respectfully disagreed.
He envisaged it as being an extremely powerful moment in the film.
Much of that power would be derived
from the sheer quantity of coffins
by the repetition of form, he explained.

Notwithstanding
we whittled the number down
—thirteen coffins
arranged in a kind of peloton
on the shiny waxed floor
so that at the golden hour
the sun would splice
just so
through the windows
fall between
the dark shapes in
long fingers of light.

The sound guy pointed out that some were in fact caskets.
He'd worked on a documentary.
The casket (rectangular) had come into vogue
by virtue of the fact that its shape
was less suggestive of the human body.
Wardrobe said women were broader
at the hips than at the shoulders
and that presumably
women died in equal numbers.
I'm no expert the sound guy said
but, whatever the reason,
the coffin and its anthropoid design tapered out.

When at last the scene was set
it felt somehow municipal—
town hall after a gunfight
horses of the corpses
still hitched outside to the rail.
Haze more haze
the cry went out—
the smoke machine affording the air itself gravitas
a girl with blue hair employed
just to press a button
on a cord around her neck,
—just to cast the pall.

In between takes
the young played dead.
The crew took turns taking photos of each other
laid out against the ivory satin.
The lighting guys in their pearl buttoned shirts
looked so handsome
thick clean hair
laying a little flat on their heads
pink chap-stick lips.
The young need no mortician—
cowboy Kens still in their cellophane boxes
playing at looking like they were "just asleep".

Yet I was discomposed
by another repetition
—the anthropoids, without exception
as they leaned back
into that other place
shut their eyes
crossed their wrists
laid their palms across their chest.
There is a brace position for death—
the hands fold
over the body and close
the shuddering wound of the heart.

The extravagant rectitude of bees

John Kinsella

The extravagant rectitude of bees
in the hollow of a middle-aged York gum:

over the decade I have fallen
before them, stung, full of regret;

membranes of x-rays,
rapid sketches of transit.

They've changed the way I see:
where they've been is always

before me. A different sense
of temperature doesn't alter

with eye-scan and aura,
with impression of avoidance—

azure of the sky and chlorophyll of canopy
reddened in the cramped darkness.

Torn abdomen, histamines.
I risk saying they are now

used to me. I slow wing
motion only to live longer

in resonant bands, blur
manna wattle pollen.

These patterns I word into fields,
smears lost in thumbprints;

autonomous as collectives,
glorious in memory of tree.

This portrait of descent,
realigning of exits

www.ingramcontent.com/pod-product-compliance
Lightning Source LLC
Chambersburg PA
CBHW020324010526
44107CB00054B/1969
9780648850496